Poetic Words

FROM THE

Heart

PATRICIA LYNN TURNER

authorHOUSE®

AuthorHouse™
1663 Liberty Drive
Bloomington, IN 47403
www.authorhouse.com
Phone: 833-262-8899

Published by AuthorHouse 11/28/2020

ISBN: 978-1-6655-0935-0 (sc)
ISBN: 978-1-6655-0934-3 (e)

Library of Congress Control Number: 2020923631

Print information available on the last page.

Contents

Prelude

Spiritual

Inspiration

Life

Relationship

Epilogue

To Dr. Begel, Alicia, Ron, Celeste, and Jackie thank you for your inspiration, your support and your well wishes.

I dedicate this book to you.

Prelude

A play on words

In my poems, you'll find that my words don't always match.
It's because your thoughts I'm trying to catch.

Although the stories will often time make sense.
But sometimes they may even, have you in suspense.

My words it's true sometimes they don't rhyme.
But just like this one, the words still are all mine.

Sometimes it's true, they are just to amuse you.
And sometimes it's cause, I didn't have a clue.

But my stories will still be a good read.
But remember my words, are always a seed.

Better place

My poetry shows my mind is in a better place.
Cause I gave people their sense of space.

I'm no longer holding on to what could have been.
Which now has helped my heart to mend.

I feel so much better, and my world has become bright.
And I now have the goal of happiness insight.

Now that I finally have let things go.
I hope my happiness can truly show.

Clear

I'll write in the morning when my mind is clear.
And my words will be sincere.

I'll write to you words that are kind.
Also, whatever words that comes to mind.

I'll try to write words that are nice.
I may even write words, that give advice.

I'll write to you in the morning, while the sun shines bright.
And hope that my words to you, are always a delight.

Glory

When you read my book, you'll learn so much about me.
Of who I am and how I am and who I have come to be.

Some of it may often time, be kind of hard to read.
And you'll find out why I needed God to intercede.

You will see my life has been, often time real strange.
It is filled with things, I somehow needed to change.

So as you read along, the poems of my life's story.
You can see what I've overcome and why I give God the glory.

Hit me up

If you find a wrong word, I used in my book.
You'll never know just how long this book took.

So if you ever find, a wrong word or a sentence or two.
I want you to know this is because this is all new.

You see I am an amateur at all this writing stuff.
So there may be a word or two that I'll miss sho'nuff.

So if you ever find that I put the wrong word there.
Hit me up and tell me cause I honestly do care.

Lovely words

Lovely words are not always my thing.
I can't always write words that shine like bling.

Sometimes my words aren't always nice.
There not always words that are sugar and spice.

My words are sometimes just thoughts in my head.
But sometimes my words are just meant to be said.

Cause sometimes my words aren't nice nor kind.
But they were just words that came to my mind.

So sometimes, I write words that doesn't make any sense.
And sometimes my words can be a little intense.

So when you read my words and they have nothing to say.
I still hope that my words managed to brighten up your day.

Lyrics

I write a lot of poetry, about so many simple things.
But most of the times its, music to me that my heart sings.

But writing is the music that plays around inside my head.
So often time the lyrics are meant to be read.

There may be many times when the lyrics are often sad and blue.
Because at that time, those lyrics are, about what I'm going through.

Sometimes I write about silly things and most of which are true.
But many times when you read along, you'll hear your heart sing too.

Sometimes you'll even read a word and anticipate my next line.
Cause sometimes my lyrics often will bring you a ray of sunshine.

I hope as you read a phrase, a simple line or two.
Some of my words will somehow encourage you.

My poetry

As you read my poetry, you will find that most of them are about me. You'll find Life and Relationship are, about the pain that wouldn't set me free.

To me, you may find that It maybe often and sometimes very hard to read.
So my poetry comes with a huge warning, so I'm asking you to take heed.

As you read along, you will find that some of my poetry may even fit your story.
But if it does, I hope that you will fight and in life have the glory.

See my life which, was so often filled with so much heartache and pain.
I can look at my life and cheer because it didn't drive me insane.

So as you read about my life and wonder whatever became of me.
I am a woman who's honestly in life has been set free.

My words

I'm a simple poet, and my poetry will show just that.
Cause I write at that time, from wherever my mind is at.

I may never use in my poems a great big word.
So often when I write, my words you've already heard.

I write whatever comes to me, so this you'll often see.
Sometimes I'll even write a poem about you and me.

So no matter what words come to me at that particular time.
They'll always speak from my heart, with words that often rhyme.

No truth

When you read my poems, the subjects are not always true.
Some are of men and things I may or may not be going through.

They are just random stories I made up in my mind.
So each of these stories, maybe just one of a kind.

Sometimes the stories of these men, can be the same.
And of how puzzling it is to be a puzzle piece in their little game.

These men are often many times, just a figment of my imagination.
To write stories of these men always gives me a sweet sensation.

These stories in my head are often time in my mind it's true.
They indeed are of men I knew and, some are of men I never knew.

You may find it hard to believe that they don't have a word of truth.
If you believe in all my stories, your mind may go through the roof.

I often sit and think of a story that maybe, to me, be a good read.
So if my story reads of realism, then I've planted in your mind a good
seed.

So when you read a story and of which appears to be real.
You may or may not figure it out and it's really no big deal.

So when you read my stories, they simply are to amuse you.
Cause it may just be a story, of which none of the words are true.

Personal

Some of my poems are personal and, this you may not know.
The anger that comes out in words, they will surely show.

You might find the words, disturbing and tough to read.
But these words are inside me, so I'm warning you to take heed.

They are of things that happened in my life and, they tell my life's story.
Some of them are stories of what happen and what truly happen to me.

I find myself often time lashing out with a word.
So most of time they'll be words, of which you may have heard.

My stories are sometimes sad and blue and, this you'll surely see.
And sometimes these sad stories, they sneak outside of me.

I try to keep these feelings away, from everyone to see.
But as you read these words they are the words that's just inside of me.

So as you read my poems, they should often come with a warning.
All I have to say for now is, maybe my words will be happier in the morning.

Place

Why do my poetry reflect on such a dark place?
I guess this is where my minds at, so it's simply the case.

I'm trying to write from another place, that's in my mind.
Cause these words I writing to you, show I'm not being kind.

I'm laughing, and I'm crying as I'm writing to you.
Cause you know these words, are simply not true.

But it's true my poems are, reflecting on my dark side.
I guess these are my true feelings, in which I cannot deny.

I guess my heart at, this time, is not filled with much joy.
All I can do is think, is boy oh boy oh boy oh boy oh boy.

And how now i have to find a way, to get some peace of mind.
So I can now find some words, that are genuinely nice and kind.

But I guess my mind is stuck right here.
Cause you're reading from my heart whose words are clear.

So I guess I have to get my heart together.
So my poems will read much better.

Pray

I'll pray over these words that you're about to read.
Cause some of these words they may plant a seed.

I'll pray that these words to you, bring a sense of hope.
And that they will be some words, to help you also cope.

I hope they'll be words, that will make you smile.
And that, that smile will stay, in your heart for a while.

I hope that the words also will be music to your ears.
And words to your heart, that don't make you shed tears.

I hope that my words to you, bring a sense of happiness.
So I hope that my words bring, a joy that you can confess.

I hope they bring to you a sense of peace to your mind.
And know that these words are always meant to be kind.

I hope these words ring with words to help you.
For it was just time that I spoke with words that are true.

I don't know what more words I should surely say.
I just hope that some of these words will brighten up your day.

Rest

I asked God to turn the words off in my head.
Because I was tired and I wanted to go to bed.

I wanted to get a night of good rest.
And thought about tomorrow, my mind I would test.

I wanted to wait to see what crazy words I'd have to say.
Something I may think of that might brighten up your day.

Cause I never know each day and the words it will bring.
But I'm ready to write new words to make your heart sing.

Sides of me

Some of my poetry shows my dark side.
A part of me, I do not hide.

I bear my soul with a simple word.
With words from me you've never heard.

There are many sides and many parts of me.
Some of them I've even let you see.

I cannot hide just who I am.
And from you my friend I will not scam.

I have shown you my good side.
Now my dark side from you I won't hide.

You have seen the good the bad and the worst of me.
Now every part of me, you now see.

There

You're bound to find yourself in my words poetry.
Cause my poetry is not always about me.

You might find yourself in one or two lines.
With words of you that are all mine.

Don't be offended when you find yourself there.
Because things about you to the world I may share.

My words are just words that I like to express.
Sometimes my words are often a hot mess.

I don't mean to offend you if you find yourself there.
Cause about you I, honestly do care.

So if you find yourself in a rhyme.
Keep in mind they're just words that are mine.

Words in my head

I can't keep up with the words in my head.
So I may not be accountable for each word I have said.

I may say a word that makes no sense to you.
But some of the words are meant to be true.

But these are the words, that dance around in my head.
I, too, may not believe a word of what I have said.

Some of these words may form a story or two.
Don't believe every word, cause some of them aren't true.

I've told you before, some of my stories are just that.
Cause those stories came from, where my mind was just at.

So take heed when you read, what I simply have said.
Cause some of them are just words that bounce around in my head.

Words

There are millions of words dancing around in my head.
I try to write them down before I go to bed.

I may not know the poem and what it's about.
I know it will be good and that I have no doubt.

The words will become a line, a sentence, or two.
The words will be special this I promise you.

I'll try to write something special to leave on your mind.
I'll try to write words that are honest, true and kind.

So as you read words, that speaks from my heart.
I hope you enjoy each word from the very start.

Spiritual

Adam and Eve

God made man first, yes this is true.
But he saw that there was more that he should do.

So he caused a deep sleep to fall upon the man.
And then he made the very first woman.

He called this man Adam and the woman he called Eve.
He placed them in the garden, where the woman was deceived.

For there was one tree, of which the fruit was forbidden.
They should have known that their sin was not hidden.

God called out to Adam and then unto Eve.
For he is the Lord, and he can't be deceived.

God said unto Adam, for listening to thy wife.
Now you can't eat, from the tree which is called life.

God multiplied Eve's sorrow, so great it would be.
So in labor her pain she surely would see.

God sent them away east of Eden to stay.
For all of their sin they surely did pay.

Advice

Today is a good day, and it's a day of sunshine.
Because my sadness, was on the decline.

I didn't feel sad, nor did I feel blue.
It was because I felt something new.

I felt a sense of joy inside.
So my happiness, did begin to rise.

I found myself smiling and smiling today.
So I believed this joy surely would stay.

So I allowed myself to enjoy this feeling.
So I got on my knees and began kneeling.

Then I thanked and thanked the Lord for this day.
And I asked him in prayer to not let this joy stray.

Then I thanked him over and over and over again.
For the joy to my heart, he did send.

I knew only he could change my heart.
And he did this, the moment my day did start.

I stayed on my knees as I continued to pray.
And I asked him in prayer, to always guide my day.

I got quiet as I began to hear the words he did say.
And he told me he'll be here always, to brighten up my day.

But he said something else he said do not again from me stray.
And he said always wait to hear his answer when I kneel to pray.

And he also said he's never late when he answers my prayer.
He also told me to have patience because he will always be there.

And from this point on, I knew my life would be nice.
So I thanked him and thanked him for his God's given advice.

Having the key

What would your world be without me?
Having me in your life is undoubtedly having the key.

You would be lost, and so all alone.
If it wasn't for me, you have known.

I was placed here in your life to save your soul.
This is and always will be my main goal.

I've given you the knowledge to preach my word.
I want you to preach it until everyone has heard.

No one should ever, not know of me.
Cause I want to be place in their hearts and forever be.

I want my people to keep heaven in their sight.
For who am I only, but the Lord Jesus Christ.

Heaven in sight

When I was young and I was just a little girl.
I've prayed for God, to change my world.

I prayed and asked God, to do this for me.
Cause In my heart, I needed God to be.

I always knew that I needed God to be there.
So I asked him to be there through prayer.

I knew that only God could change my world.
And I knew this from the time I was a young girl.

You see I was taught to believe in God.
And I always knew God wasn't a façade.

I knew God wasn't a figment of my imagination.
So I could praise him with joy and elation.

I knew for sure I could trust him.
And adding him, my light wouldn't be dim.

So I thanked God for allowing, my light to shine bright.
And I thanked him for giving me a chance to have heaven in sight.

Instilled

What God instilled in you is to be a good man.
And you are doing good and the best that you can.

I know God smiles when he looks down upon you.
Because you are doing what he expects you to do.

You are living your life according to God's plan.
I know that you are indeed a God's fearing man.

God knows that you worship him with love that is true.
I want you to know God is so proud of you.

Praising you Lord

Lord I praise you, with my mind that is clear.
So my love for you, is so sincere.

I praise you with my heart that is clean.
So as I praise you, every word do I mean.

Lord, I lift my hands high up to you.
No matter what, I am going through.

Lord, I praise you with every breath that I take.
And you Lord, I will never forsake.

Lord, I'll praise you for you're always there.
Thank you Lord, for your love and care.

Spice of life

Jesus is the spice of life and he's the one who adds the flavor.

So when you need a little flavor look to Jesus our Lord and savior.

Steps

Dear Lord guide my feet with every step I make.
And so as I walk, I don't make a mistake.

I cannot walk in this life all alone.
Please guide my feet as I walk the unknown.

Lord, I need you to walk with me every day of my life.
And teach me how to walk with no envy or strife.

Lord, I know I can do all things through you.
So trusting in you is something I will do.

Dear Lord, always stay by my side, as I continue to walk.
And please continue to listen to me as I walk and talk.

I need you, dear Lord, to always stay by my side.
And I'll walk with you, with honor and pride.

Lord, I want you to know I do love you.
And thank you for loving me and showing me you do.

I want to thank you Lord, for guiding each step that I take.
And thank you Lord, for showing me, me you will not forsake.

Thank you Lord

I count on you every day.
To walk before me and pave my way.

I count on you when things get tough.
I count on you, so very much.

I try so hard to stand on my faith.
And to understand that, you're never late.

I count on you to see me through.
I really do depend on you.

I know that you've, always been there.
To show me that you always care.

I want you to know, I appreciate you.
Thank you, Lord, for everything you do.

Inspiration

Best me

I'm living my life and loving it.
Cause I no longer feel like a misfit.

I have finally found my way.
And I'm now looking forward to each day.

Cause I see the beauty of my world.
And I see it as a beautiful oyster's pearl.

I've come to realize I'm living my best.
And I have overcome every test.

I now see I've become the best me.
Cause I have become who I'm supposed to be.

Cause I'm living my life as this beautiful me.
And how beautiful I am I surely see.

I see the beautiful person I've become.
Cause I'm no longer am feeling numb.

And I know who I am and this is so true.
Now I'm living and loving my life as I'm supposed too.

Better days

How are you truly doing today?
I hope that you are doing ok.

I know that you are feeling sad and blue.
Just know one thing I am here for you.

You know seeing you sad seems so out of place.
Because your the one who always has a smile on your face.

You know I wish I had word to ease your pain and sorrow.
But brighter days will be here as soon as tomorrow.

So try not to cry, worry or, be sad or blue.
And know this is something God will bring you through.

Big girl

You've always been a smart, intelligent big girl.
Cause you've had faith to step out in this world.

You have always managed to do things well.
And you seemed to do things that make you excel.

You have always managed to do your very best.
And sometimes you done it without giving life some rest.

You can be anything you want to in this world.
Cause you will always be a smart big girl.

Bold

I'll see you through it, and I'll even hold your hand.
Together we will make a very bold stand.

You can get through this, even though these times may be rough.
I won't let you fall now that times seems so tough.

I'll be here to help you, no matter how much.
Cause I want you to know, it's my heart that you touch.

So now is the time I need to rally around you.
Cause you'll get past this cause, I'll help you through.

So don't take your eyes now off of the finish line.
Cause you will reach there in, just a matter of time.

So continue to reach for the sky and be bold.
Cause it's in the end, it's the prize you will hold.

I'm proud of you for being someone who does fight.
Yet I know for you things will turn out just right.

I will always be here to hold on to your hand.
But it will be you that makes the very bold stand.

Cause you've always managed when life seems to unfold.
So be very proud of yourself cause you have always been bold.

Challenges

I can write you a poem every single day.
I may not know the words it may come to say.

It might even be just a word or a couple of lines or two.
To deliver some gentle words of encouragement to you.

To these words at this time to you, you may not even come to relate.
But you'll remember my words when you have too much on your plate.

But I'll tell you this one thing and this I hope you know.
That God is always with you, and this, I know, is so.

So I'm telling you there are no challenge God won't see you through.
And for you there is nothing in this world that God won't do for you.

Change

Today maybe the day, to change your life.
Cause today you'll have, a new vision is sight.

Today your goal will be something new.
Maybe today will be a new dream come true.

Whatever this new day, it will bring a new sun.
And I hope in your journey, you'll continue to run.

So just enjoy whatever it will bring.
And I pray to your life, it will bring a good thing.

Delight

When I look at you, I see a ray of sunlight.
I see someone whose smile always does delight

I see someone that makes the world go round.
I see someone when I look at who never wears a frown.

I see someone who so often manages to smile.
I see someone whose smile you can see from a mile.

I see someone whose an absolute delight.
I see someone whose joy is always a sight.

I see someone whose smile will always shine bright.
I see someone who is genuinely an absolute delight.

Despair

You'll often find yourself in times of despair.
That's the time you should know that God is truly there.

You may not, at times, reach God's outstretched hand.
But he is truly there asking you to take a stand.

He's at that time asking you to stand on his word.
But it's at this time you'll fall short on what you've heard.

God is there to help but you won't feel like he's there.
But his loving arms are around you to show he does care.

So when you find yourself in times of trouble and your life's in despair.
That's the time you should trust and know God is truly there.

Disarray

Why is your heart in such disarray?
Don't you know that God always makes a way?

Things may happen, that you don't quite understand.
But remember, God above always has a plan

There's nothing that he doesn't know or see.
So when things happen just let them be.

So why oh why are you in such disarray?
Just remember this one thing God always makes a way.

Do not wallow

Get those thoughts out of your head.
Then climb yourself right out of that bed.

There's a big ole world waiting here for you.
Cause there's so much in it, you can do.

So don't wallow in self -pity get rid of that pain.
Cause that self- pity can truly drive you insane.

You see, there is so much more to life for you to see.
So get that pain out your heart and fine you will be.

Cause there is so much more to life for you to explore.
Go on set yourself free so your heart can now soar.

Go on with your life and set yourself free.
Cause now there's a place of happiness for you to be.

Go ahead, step out on faith into this great big ole world.
Cause God gave you the strength to now be a big girl.

And now, since you have been set free from your pain.
Do thank God for the joys of life that now rain.

Encouragement

Let me write to you my love.
With the pure love from the heavens above.

With words that are meant to encourage you.
To help you along with what you are going through.

I am reaching out to you with an extended hand.
Through this time in which you don't understand.

I completely understand and I feel your pain.
With this loss it will take time for the strength you'll regain.

No one expects you to carry such a heavy load.
You'll need your friends and family as you travel this dark road.

I know this time isn't for you simply the best.
But what you need now is time for your heart to rest.

Whatever you need I'll be here for you.
To help you through whatever you're going through.

I know I can't remove from your heart it's sorrow.
But I'll pray that you'll have a better day tomorrow.

Fallen

You've always seemed to stand tall.
So you never imagined you would fall.

But hold on cause tomorrow is another day.
And you can look forward to paving your own way.

But in case you need strength, ask for it when you pray.
And you'll get the strength from God right away.

So get up move, on and once again continue to fight.
Cause knowing your prayers will make things alright.

So get up, keep on forging ahead and again stand tall.
Cause you were not meant to stay down when you fall.

Fight

Don't you know you have the courage to fight?
Don't you know standing up is honestly your right?

So why are you just staying stuck there?
Go on and move on so that pain you won't bear.

Don't just stand still and give up the fight.
Continue to fight it's your God given right.

Why have you stood there throwing in the towel?
Don't stand there, pretending that you're not in denial.

I'm telling you, you got to move on and forge ahead.
And don't worry about the tears you may shed.

I'm only speaking to you because I care.
Don't you know you don't have to be stuck there?

O.k. come on, get moving, and move on with your life.
Don't let that pain fill your heart with strife.

I'm telling you I see your courage, so continue to fight.
So keep on fighting and fight with all of your might.

Fly high

You were made to soar so fly high as the sky.
You can reach to higher heights, so go ahead and fly.

Now go on, set yourself for a much higher height.
Cause you can reach any goal, you have insight.

So keep on flying to fulfill all your dreams.
Cause, your reality, is to fly high by all means.

So continue to fly high cause you will not fall.
So go on fly high and just have a ball.

So keep on flying high till you reach a new height.
And continue to reach every goal in your sight.

Get up

Get up little girl why are you still laying there?
Don't you know you have people that care?

Don't stay laying there being filled with that pain.
You have to get up cause you have so much to gain.

Get up little girl we are all here for you.
Come on little girl, get up we'll all see you through.

Get up little girl, and face this big ole world.
You got to get up it's time for you to be a big girl.

Get up little girl don't continue lying there.
Cause all that pain alone you don't have to bear.

Get up little girl, and we will all hold your hand.
Get up little girl, and together we'll help you to stand.

Hiding

Why are you hiding in this world?
Why do you need to hide in this world little girl?

Why don't you want the world to see you?
Cause hiding is something you always do.

Why do you always hide in this world?
Why must you keep hiding in this world little girl?

Stop hiding and let the world see who you are.
And the world will see you and that you are truly a star.

So come out from hiding show your face to the world.
And the world will see that you are a beautiful little girl.

I may not know

I may not know what you are going through.
I may not even have a clue.

I may not have seen you in a while.
I hope that you are still wearing a smile.

I don't know why I am writing you this.
I guess it's because in my heart it's you that I miss.

I just want you to know I am still on your team.
And I can only hope that you are still living your dream.

Whatever the reasons, you are reading this.
I want you to know I'm sending my love along with a kiss.

Kind words

If I could write you a few kind words.
They'll be words that you've already heard.

These words would be that I love you.
These three words are words that are oh so true.

Then If I could say a little more.
I'd say you are truly someone I adore.

All these words to comfort you.
And how I feel I hope you knew.

My words are word just to remind you.
Of my love so genuine and true.

Let go

Why is your heart filled with that pain?
Do you want that pain in your heart to remain?

You got to find a way to get rid of it.
Just let it go cause in your heart, it can't fit.

I know you know you can make it go away.
You don't have to be ruled by it every day.

You have to find a way to make that pain go away.
Cause it must leave your heart cause it cannot stay.

Just believe in your heart that you have let that pain go.
Then when those feelings come back you can tell them no, no.

Little star

What are you running from you keep running little star?
Don't you know when you run you won't get very far?

Why are you running? are you running from your past?
Don't you know I see your sorrow that won't forever last?

Why do you keep running when it won't get you very far?
You have to stop running, so stop running little star.

Why are you running when things can and will get better?
I see your sorrow wrapped around you as if it is a sweater.

I think that you need to take time to walk so in life you will get far.
So when are you going to stop running, stop running little star?

Mirror

When I look in the mirror who do I see?
I see a beautiful woman staring back at me.

When I look at this woman and I wonder who is she?
All I can see is this woman being the best she can be.

Then when I imagine this woman being her best.
I see a woman who has exceeded life's test.

When I look in the mirror who do I see.
I see a beautiful woman being the best she can be.

Mirror's image

I see a lot of you in me.
That is why I won't let you be.

I know that you have the spirit to fight.
So I know that you can see what is right.

I know that you know you can depend on yourself.
When it comes to fighting, you need no one's help.

You see, I see you for who you are and who you are meant to be.
I know who you are because when I'm looking at you, I'm looking at me.

No matter the cost

Why are you crying my, precious and dear friend?
Whatever the problem, is I'll be there in the end.

Why do you feel so lost and alone?
I'm here to help you face the unknown.

So why do you feel like you need to run away?
I'm telling you, I'm here for you every day.

I can only help you if you let me in.
I am here for you, my precious dear friend.

Why do you feel like, for you, no one does care?
I'm telling you now I will always be there.

So what is the problem what's going on with you?
Whatever it, is I will be there to see you through.

So don't stand there crying and feeling lost.
I will be there for you no matter the cost.

So stop crying and wipe those tears from your eyes.
Together will get through this I tell you no lies.

Plant your feet

Stand there, be still, and plant your feet.
Don't feel like when things go wrong you can't stand the heat.

You have the tools to handle what you're going through.
You have to trust in God, and this is something you must do.

Don't stand there wavering just stand still for God's sake.
Don't you know that God will be there and he's never too late?

So keep your feet planted and stand on solid ground.
Cause you may not be able to see God but he's always around.

Don't you know sometimes your faith will be put through a test?
Just know when you come through, you'll be better than your best.

So when you feel your knees wobbling and you begin to fall.
Just stand on God's words and you'll be able to stand tall.

So don't weave and wobble as you walk in your faith.
Just know sometimes you will make a mistake.

So as you walk in your faith, remember to plant your feet.
And remember in times of trouble you can stand the heat.

Simple words

These simple little words are coming from me.
And they are words of encouragement I share with thee.

They are words to tell you to always be kind.
And let the words of love come from your heart, soul, and mind.

And let them always be words to show that you care.
And to your friends and loved ones you'll always be there.

And always take time to send them best wishes.
And most of all don't forget to send hugs and kisses.

Smile

We laughed so much together I'd thought you'd stay for a while.
But in the meantime, you've managed to bring back my smile.

You brought back to my life the lost happiness.
Cause my life was honestly just a big mess.

I never expected in life this sudden change.
Cause when I looked at my life it was simply strange.

You see you've brought to my life so many good things.
Now to my heart, joy, and happiness, it now sings.

I'd never believed my world couldn't be so blue.
And it's because of the joy you bring only something you could do.

Speak up

Speak up young man and use your voice.
Cause staying silent is not a wise choice.

Speak up, young man, and say a word.
Don't stand there in silence and let your voice be unheard.

Cause thinking the world is not listening is absurd.
So you have to speak up so your voice will be heard.

So speak up young man, the world will listen when you talk.
You have to speak up and in this world leave your mark.

Don't stand there in silence, being an invisible young man.
Stand up, speak your words, and just take a stand.

Speak up young man and use your loud voice.
Cause staying silent in never a wise choice.

You have to speak up and speak words that are true.
Speak up, be a man, and the world will hear you.

Speak

Speak your mind and get things off your chest.
Then you'll realize you'll feel better than the best.

Cause holding things inside can get the best of you.
So speak about your feelings with words that are true.

Never silence yourself and become shut down.
So talk about your feelings with words that are sound.

Speak about your feelings to people who care.
And to all the people whose shown you there, there.

So never let yourself keep your feelings inside.
Always remember it's your feelings and not your pride.

So if you ever feel like you need to speak your mind.
Do it with strength and with words that are kind.

Star

This is for the little girl who knew nothing but pain.
I'm so proud of you for letting nothing drive you insane.

You could have let your problems get the best of you.
In spite of everything, you managed to push through.

You were not supposed to crumble and not even to fall.
Good for you, little girl, for always standing tall.

You hung on with all that you knew and all that you had.
Even though sometimes things seem like they would drive you mad.

So always be very proud of who you are.
Cause you are now a woman who is truly a shining star.

Stop

Stop living in pain and sorrow and stop wasting your tears.
Cause your heart will stay sad, so it's time to switch gears.

Cause dwelling on your pain and sorrow will keep you in pain.
If you don't watch out it could drive you insane.

Forget about your sorrow and let those things go.
Then you'll be filled with happiness, and the joy will show.

Aren't you tired of holding on to that mess?
Let those pains go so your life can be its best.

You know sometimes we become stuck living in our past.
So all of that pain and sorrow will continue to last.

So I'll give you advice cause this is something you should know.
Stop dwelling on your past sorrows and let them things go.

Tears

Wipe those tears from your eye's you don't have to cry.
Cause I am here for you with a love that your heart can't deny.

You see I, will see you through whatever's bothering you.
I'll be there with love to help see you through.

So you don't have to worry, so get those things off your chest.
Cause I am here to help you so you'll feel better than your best.

So wipe away those tears that are falling on your face.
And let some love from my heart fill your heart's space.

So don't think that no one truly cares about you.
I am here with love for you so that is not true.

Tough

Put a smile on your face don't be so sad.
Why in the world do you think things are all bad?

Don't you know that things will be alright?
All you have to do is continue to fight.

Cause you are stronger than you'll ever know.
Don't you know your strength surely does show?

So keep your head up and look toward the sky.
And then don't ask yourself the reasons why.

Cause things aren't as they seem and you have a reason to smile.
If you look at the positives, your smile will last for a while.

So don't be stuck there being blue and all sad.
Cause you have 101 reasons to be happy and glad.

So wipe those tears that are falling from your face.
And continue to run well the hurdles of life's race.

You will get through this cause you are tough.
Just know in this life things won't always be rough.

So again keep your head up and look toward the sky.
And don't worry about the tears you may have to cry.

So don't be so down and think times will always be rough.
just depend on your strength cause you are tough.

Well, well

Well, well look at you I see you over there looking all cute.
What are you up to looking all good as if you're in a photoshoot?

Why are you over there looking so fine?
You'll have people looking at you and thinking you're a dime.

I see your beauty that also comes from deep within.
People will see your beauty and they'll want to be your friend.

Cause your beauty is a rarity as rare as a bottle of wine.
You are so beautiful you should come with a warning sign.

You see you turn heads when your walking down the street.
And you're leaving an impression on the people that you meet.

Well, well I see you over there really looking all sweet.
When people stop and talk to you they'll get a sweet treat.

So don't change how you look and change who you are.
Just know when people see your beauty, they'll see you're a star.

What's the deal

Be honest about your feeling and say how you feel.
And then talk about your feelings and just keep them real.

Be a man about yours and speak with words how you feel.
Speak about your feeling with words that won't kill.

Just be honest with your words and say what is real.
So open your heart to me and say how you feel.

I will get your heart's message if you speak what is real.
You are a smart man so use your words what's the big deal.

So come on speak from your heart the words that are real.
And then when you, speak I will know how you feel.

When I grow up

When I grow up what will I be?
And when I do who will you see?

Will you see the real me?
When I grow up what will I be.

When I grow up I hope you'll see.
The person I am and who I'm inspired to be.

So when I grow up I hope you'll like me.
And I hope that you'll like who I've come to be.

When I grow up I will always be me.
This beautiful person you love and see.

When I grow up I will be.
The very best person that is in me.

Who are you?

Who are you this person that I see?
Cause you surely are who you are meant to be.

I see you over there standing so very tall.
And I've seen you get up every time you fall.

You will do great things in this magnificent world.
Cause you are really a smart and beautiful girl.

You can be proud when you've reached a goal.
Cause you truly do have a fighting soul.

You've already shown that you are tough.
Cause you have shown to this world so very much.

So continue to strive and let your light shine bright.
And remember always you have the strength to fight.

Who I AM

I'd like for you to walk a mile in my shoes.
Then ask yourself whose life would you choose.

After walking that mile, then you'll see.
Just how I have come to be.

Then maybe you will stop judging me.
Cause who I am is who you can't see.

My life may not have always been the best.
But I can say I've withstood every test.

I may not be who you expect me to be.
But I will not stand there and let you judge me.

I may not be to you a person whose life is right.
But who I am and what I stand for I'll continue to fight.

So the next time you stand there in judgment of me.
Remember, it's my life, so just let me be.

Cause I will not ever try to tell you who you are.
But I'll tell you this I AM a shining star.

You are amazing

You are an amazing person.
Just look at everything you have done.

No one could do any better than you.
You always stand out no matter what you do.

You should be so proud of how much you've done.
And you've overcome every obstacle under the sun.

You can look at your life and count all your blessing.
And you have also done things to show you're a king.

So continue to shine and keep forging ahead.
And be thankful for all the tears of joy you have shed.

So when you look back and everything you've done.
Be proud of yourself cause you are an amazing son.

You can do it

I know all about you, so I know just how you feel.
I hear you talk about your feelings that are oh so real.

I've seen you overcome in life so very much.
And you have used nothing as a crutch.

You've managed to do things with no one's help.
I'm proud of you for doing things all by yourself.

You see you are strong and able to do it alone.
You have the strength and this you have shown.

But you can't do this, you'll have my shoulder to lean on.
But I know you can do this and this is well known.

Just be vigilant while you are dealing with all this.
And know that my prayers are with you and they come with a kiss.

Young man

Young man, young man, don't let anger fill your heart.
You cannot do that cause you're much to smart.

Don't let that anger get the best of you.
That's isn't something you want to do.

Young man, young man you have to let that anger go.
Or that anger inside you will always show.

There is no good reason to hold on to such anger.
Cause holding on to that anger puts your heart in danger.

Young man, young man, take heed to this advice.
Letting go of that anger will make your life nice.

Young man, young man, you can let that anger go.
Then you can let your true happiness show.

Young man, young man you have the strength to be wise.
Letting go of that anger is like winning life's prize.

Young man, young man, if you let that anger go.
Then you'll always let your true happiness show.

Your world

Your world can be a better place.
If you choose differently how to run life's race.

You can change the way you choose to run.
You can choose wisely and make life fun.

You don't have to make your life a difficult thing.
You can choose a way to make your heart sing.

You can make decisions and life will work out.
Then through the roof joy from wisdom you'll shout.

So just realize it's how you choose to live in this world.
Will determine if you can give life a twirl.

Cause your world can be a beautiful thing.
If you let it, it can truly make your heart sing.

Life

A mother's warning

My mother warned me about men like you.
And what she warned me about was more than true.

She said to me you wouldn't be a good man.
But her warnings I didn't want to understand.

But her words turned out to be words that are right.
Cause all you ever want to do is argue and fight.

And now her warnings ring with words that are true.
So with you, I'm confused about what to do.

I know in my head is saying I can do better that you.
But my heart doesn't want for us to be through.

I don't like feeling beatdown and confused.
But by you I just feel often time used.

Cause I never thought I'd be in a relationship like this.
But if I get the strength to leave you, it's you I won't miss.

You see my mother's words are dancing around in my head.
And I so many times wished I would have listened to what she had said.

You see sometimes a mother's warnings can be right about men.
Cause they can tell when a man won't be a good lover or a good friend.

A true friend

When times get rough, and my cross seems too hard to bear.
You've shown me time and time again you do care.

Grateful and thankful to you is this message I send.
I truly appreciate you my good and dear friend.

All I ever wanted

Pain, then abuse is all I know.
So the pain of my life surely does show.

Pain that comes from when I was a child.
Then as an adult, here came abuse to stay for a while.

No one taught me that these things weren't o.k.
So I thought things were normal in every way.

No I wasn't often time whooped when I was a child.
But not knowing that I was love didn't make me smile.

Throughout my adult life, I've lived with some form of abuse.
But with these men for their behavior I'd make an excuse.

I went from the pain of my childhood to being treated unkindly by men.
When all I ever wanted was for my lover to also be my friend.

Battles

Why are you standing there not fighting and being so still?
Don't you know you have to keep moving so what is the deal?

Why are you standing there not putting up a fight?
Why are you there not fighting with all of your might?

You have to fight your battles so keep moving and fight.
Don't lose out on life's battles cause fighting is your right.

So my friend do fight and fight with all of your might.
Then in your life things will turn out alright.

So don't stand there being stuck in one place.
Continue to fight and your battles and them you can ace.

You see your, battles can be won only by you.
So standing there and fighting you surely must do.

Then you'll come out the victor when your battles are all won.
And then you can cheer loudly when it's all said and done.

Best friend

In my poems, you'll learn all about me.
And how I truly have come to be.

It started when I was a little child.
And a child who often had no reason to smile.

I had one friend Jackie who loved me and gave me hope.
And with the love of this best friend with life, I could cope.

No one knew of my sadness not even her my, best friend.
But the message of her love was always there in the end.

I had many days wallowing in my pain and sorrow.
But I knew because of my best friend I'd have a better day tomorrow.

Cause I was a child whose life was full of sadness and pain.
I'm telling if it wasn't for this friend I'd have no happiness to gain.

Not even my mother truly knew me as a child well.
Cause on me as a child all the lies people would tell.

I had no father in my life, so with him, I had no dealings.
So I learned early on how to mask all of my feelings.

But I knew I had one person to show that she did care.
And this best friend Jackie always showed she'd be there.

This friend doesn't know how her love saved my life.
Cause she was there through the troubling times when I had no insight.

I'm telling you this best friend love was like no other.
Cause there were times when I couldn't rely on my own mother.

This best friend was the best friend in the whole world.
Cause she truly saved my life when I was a little girl.

Best friends the aftermath

Once again, I wrote a poem to you without knowing.
And with these words where I was going.

I wrote this poem, and it made me cry.
And as I wrote these words, I didn't wonder why.

I wrote it to my very best friend.
The one who often helped my heart mend.

I had to send to her this poem I wrote for her.
I was hoping as she read, the meaning of love would occur.

I don't know why she was so heavy on my mind.
I guess it's because, to me she has always been kind.

I then sat here, fighting back the tears I tried to hide.
But deep down, I was truly crying inside.

Then after a while, my phone began to ring.
And it was from her, so the joy from my heart did sing.

Cause I hadn't heard from her in a while.
So hearing her voice did make my heart smile.

I could tell she had been touched by what she read.
Because she didn't know those feelings were lurking in my head.

As we talked on the phone, we did express how we feel.
We told each other of our feelings that were oh so real.

Just as we were getting ready to hang up, she began again to cry.
It was because we hadn't seen each other, and we didn't know why.

We made plans to see each other cause were still too each other a friend.
And the truly meaning of love to each other's heart did surely transcend.

Betrayal

Betrayal cuts deep as it can truly ruin one's life.
Betrayal is fueled by mostly envy and strife.

Betrayal in reality, can cut you real deep.
And how betrayed you can be by the secrets it can keep.

Betrayal has hidden lies within to come unfold.
And it also has secrets that are never told.

Betrayal cares for no one or its boundary.
And it can betray you and it can even betray me.

Betrayal can really ruin one's life.
Cause it can cut you by using a knife.

Betrayal has no respect for a person.
All it knows it to hurt you when it's all done.

Don't give a person who betrayed you a second chance.
Don't even give them a second glance.

Don't let being betrayed get the best of you.
Just be with the person who betrays you just through.

Bingo

One thing about me you should know.
Is I'm a person who loves bingo.

So if you're looking and you can't find me.
It's at bingo I probably will be.

I'm not a person who loves to go.
I'm there so I can yell bingo.

I'm most likely there with a good friend.
So don't bother me cause I'm trying to win.

So if you're looking and you can't find me.
Off at bingo I'll most likely be.

Blessed wishes

You've helped me out a lot through the years.
You even helped me get over my fears.

You've often told me things would be alright.
You even told me to continue to fight.

You have been there when I had no belief in myself.
Your encouraging words have always seemed to help.

And if it weren't for you, I wouldn't be where I am today.
Thank you for each kind word you did say.

I am here in this place in life because of you.
Thank you so much for always seeing me through.

I couldn't have gotten here without your support.
Without your help my life would be out of sort.

You've managed to know just what to say.
So I'm thankful for you always each day.

I can't honestly thank you enough.
Cause you were here when things were rough.

Now if I could have one more thing to say.
It'll be I'm sending blessed wishes your way.

Boy be a man

Boy, why aren't you standing up and being a man?
Why don't you in life ever have a plan?

Boy, why would you go out there and create another child?
When you know you haven't seen your other children in a while.

Boy, you sho'll are doing things that aren't truly real smart.
And this I'm telling you is coming from my heart,

Boy, you need to make better choices better decisions for your life.
I'm telling you this before a woman cuts you with a knife.

Boy, you have no clue what life's really about.
This I for sure honestly 100 percent have no doubt.

I'm telling you better get wise and stand up and be a man.
Cause when one of those baby mamas cut you, you'll finally understand.

Broken hearted

How long does it take a heart to heal?
Cause my heart's broken and it is still ill.

My heart sick, and so is my mind.
When it will be healed it's not showing a sign.

How long does it take a broken heart to heal?
Please someone can you, tell me the real.

My heart is broken, and the pain cuts deep.
Is this my world, and this pain I shall keep?

Can this broken heart be the end of me?
Tell me this in not how it's going to be.

Is this now the reality of which I will live?
It cannot cause I still have more love to give.

Broken

In the race of life, your heart will get broken and broken and broken. And for this race of broken- heartedness you won't get a trophy not even a token.

All you'll have gotten in life is some pain and heartaches. It makes you wonder about love and how you could make so many mistakes.

You'll then begin to question the decisions that you make. And you'll wonder how much more of life's heartaches can you take.

You'll wonder if your heart gets broken again will it ever heal. And if you can protect your heart by simply placing on it a seal.

You can't help but wonder why life comes with such heartaches. And what will you ever learn from making so many mistakes.

You know, with ever heartache there's a lesson to be learn. But you look forward to a new lesson without an ounce of concern.

Care

I wonder if you even know or even if you care.
About all the pain and suffering that you have now made me bear.

Cherish

I would be lost and alone without you.
I just would not know what to do.

Your friendship has come to me right on time.
And I'm sure glad I have made it mine.

Your friendship means the world to me.
Cause happiness now is all I see.

I'll cherish you forever, my beautiful friend.
And our friendship will never come to an end.

Child

I was a very unhappy child.
And for this reason, my heart didn't smile

I masked the pain of my unhappy heart.
So it seemed to me like I was smart.

No one knew the pain my heart was in.
No one knew not even my one true friend.

I hid it from her and she knew me well.
I couldn't speak up so there was no one I would tell.

I kept things to myself so my pain I did hide.
But I was feeling hurt, and I kept those feelings inside.

I was a child who seemed to get teased a lot.
But to stand up for myself I did not.

I was a child living in much pain.
I often wondered would I be truly sane.

I knew no one else you lived in pain like me.
Cause I often looked at other's life and no pain did I see.

I was just a child who felt so all alone.
I wish I had spoken up so someone else would have known.

I was a child that the true me no one knew.
Cause no one knew what I was going through.

I was the child that felt I was never good enough.
So the existence of my life was often times tough.

Now I am the person who before you still bears that pain.
And often ask myself how my childhood didn't drive me insane.

I often sit back and think about my childhood.
And the true facts of my childhood is it was no good.

But I am now this person who has to let go of my past.
Cause I now have the choice to make my happiness last.

I am and have always been the strongest person that I know.
Because of all the years I suffered my pain didn't show.

You see the pain of my childhood didn't get the best of me.
Cause I am standing strong in life and my happiness you're able to see.

So the little child who felt so unloved and all alone.
She doesn't exist anymore cause those feelings are now gone.

Daddy

This man I called daddy him I've never known.
His true feelings for me he has always shown.

He's always showed me he didn't care.
Cause in my life he has never been there.

I know such little about him, just mainly his name.
Cause to see how I was doing, he never came.

I've wondered how he could move on with his life.
You see he divorced my mon and then took another wife.

I guess forgetting about me was easy for him to do.
He never cared about me, and this is so true.

He left me a child, with so many questions to ask.
And he made me a little child whose pain I did mask.

I was a child whose mother also became her father.
Cause this man I call daddy with me he didn't bother.

Dark

Why are you hiding, hiding there in the dark?
Don't you know I see you and I can hear you when you talk?

You see you don't' hide very well, very well there in the dark.
I'll tell you, again and again, I can hear you when you talk.

I see you're trying so very hard to dim my light.
You can't dim my light cause my light is too bright.

So why are you still hiding there, hiding there in the dark?
I'll show you once and for all you can't put out my spark.

So I'll put an end to you hiding there, hiding there in the dark.
And they'll be no more whispering from you when you begin to talk.

I'll turn off all the images of you that are simply in my head.
And I'll put you to rest and won't listen to a word that you've said.

So come out of hiding and appear in plain sight.
Cause I won't give up the battle of fighting you with all my might.

Darkness lurking

I see you lurking in the shadows, the darkness of my past.
I'm trying to forget about you and your aftermath.

Why are you still lurking there trying to reveal my pain?
Why are you still lurking there what do you have to gain?

Why are you there taunting me with the memories of my past?
I keep you hidden from plain sight so your images will not last.

I see you there peeking out from the shadows of my mind.
I see that you're still lurking there with memories that are not kind.

Why are you still hiding there deep inside my head?
When I am trying very hard to put those dark memories to bed.

Why are you trying so hard to bring the darkness out of me?
When I am trying hard to make new memories why won't you just let me be?

Darkness

What's that lurking in the darkness but the memories of my past.
Nightmares of what use to be that always seems to last.

The pain of my experiences that never strays from my heart and mind.
Always in the shadows are things that were done to me that were not kind.

These things that are always lurking sometimes gets the best of me.
Cause from my heart and mind I feel like I am never free.

How do I erase the pain from a very sad existence?
Cause having darkness in my life just doesn't make any sense.

There's got to be a point in time that I didn't shed a tear.
I'm trying to figure out when the darkness wasn't here.

No one would believe that I live by the darkness of my past.
Cause the darkness of my past has come to forever last.

So the dark and gloomy memories there that's always seems to show.
Has changed me into this beautiful person that you have come to know.

Excel

One day I will no longer care what people think of me.
Then I will be me and totally set free.

To think of who I am and who I want to be.
And to only think about what is right for me.

I know who I am, and I can think for myself.
Cause I no longer have put my thoughts upon the shelf.

Cause I am now able to stand up and on my own.
Cause who I am and who I will be I have truly shown.

I am strong and I have the strength and I will not fail.
Because I am and will be the person whose life will excel.

You see I have the strength to stand alone all by myself.
Cause I am no longer willing to put my thoughts upon the shelf.

So from now on you will see I am truly a success.
And you will see I am strong and my life is not a mess.

Eyes

What's behind those piercing, those piercing eyes.
And are those piercing eyes, eyes that cannot tell lies?

What is the story of those eyes that are untold?
What is the story that those eyes hold?

What is behind those eyes I cannot see?
Can you, will you begin to tell me?

What's behind those eyes I'd like to know?
What's behind those eyes that does not show?

Those eyes, those eyes they seem to tell a story.
What's behind those eyes what is their mystery?

Those eyes they do seem to have a piercing glare.
Those eyes, those eyes that always seem to stare.

Those eyes, those eyes that have a story to share.
Those eyes can tell their story and the world will care.

What's behind those eyes peering out at me?
And what to the world will their story be?

Father

Who should I call father?
Is it the man with me who didn't bother?

Who should I call dad?
The man that only makes me sad.

Why should I call you a parent?
When your dislike for me was apparent.

Why must I morn and cry for you?
When nothing for me you would do.

Why should I have tears to cry for you?
And why is it I'm expected too.

Why is it wrong for me to feel this way?
When were you ever here for me, for a single day?

Why should I be told I have to forgive you?
When my life was full of pain and of which you had no clue.

Why should I not be allowed to feel exactly how I feel?
I have lost nothing with you dying and this is for real.

I cannot morn and cry for you the father I never knew.
So let me have my feelings because they're genuine and true.

I have to allow myself time for forgiveness as if I ever can.
Cause you were never a father, not even a stand-up man.

So these are the reasons I have no forgiveness inside my heart.
Cause these feelings start way back from the moment my life did start.

You couldn't keep up the pretense that you loved me as a child.
Cause the pretense of you loving me lasted only for a little while.

So I won't pretend now that you meant so much to me.
Cause how I feel about you the whole world can now see.

Finding love

I'll find love again with someone new.
Well, I know this cause we are through.

I'll find love cause the world's filled with men.
I'll find a man who'll be to me a friend.

I'll find love again and this I know is true.
And a love that will be something new.

I'll find love again, and this time it will be real.
And on my heart they'll place their seal.

So I'm looking forward to the love I will find.
A love to my heart it will show that it's kind

Free

When you are an unloved child, and your heart knows no love and joy.
Love seems to play games with your heart and mind as if you are a toy.

The thoughts of being unloved never seem to go away.
These feelings seem to haunt you every single day.

It doesn't matter how hard you try to change how you are feeling.
These feelings are always there in your heart, and there is no healing.

You often try to convince yourself that these feelings are untrue.
So you often ask yourself what changes must I do.

You try many things to change, just how you are feeling.
But you never find a way to get yourself to a place of healing.

You even talk to friends and family who had shown you that they care.
Cause the pain of being an unhappy child so often hard to bear.

These feelings seem to harbor a place deep inside your soul.
You begin to wonder would you harbor these feelings as you grow old.

Cause you are that little child inside whose unhappiness bears much pain.
So you ask yourself, what must you do so you'll have happiness to gain?

Cause as you grow up you wonder if you'll ever be free from that child.
The child who lurks inside your heart who never seemed to smile.

All you like is to be free from the pain your childhood brought to you.
So you keep on asking yourself what in the world must I do.

To free that little child whose buried deep inside your heart.
How can you free yourself so your healing can begin to start?

Cause you want to free yourself from that child who cries within.
Cause you don't know what to do to get your heart to mend.

All you want is for that child to grow up and free herself from pain.
Before she lets that pain make her shed tears that fall like rain.

Frightened

There was a little girl who was scared of this world.
She was scared to give life a twirl.

She didn't know why this world frightened her so much.
She just knew she felt so out of touch.

She let know one know about her fear.
So she let no one, no one come near.

You see she never had a place in this world.
Cause she was just a frightened little girl.

She felt like this world was a big ole space.
And in this world she couldn't find her place.

So she walked in this world feeling so all alone.
And these feeling was all that she had known.

Till one particular day she woke up and said.
I must get these feelings out of my head.

So she took a new approach to this world.
And decided now she must be a big girl.

So this big ole world no longer frightens her.
Cause the strength she needed did manage to occur.

So she now walks in this world with her head held high.
And asked herself why she was so frightened why.

Gloomy day

It's a dark and gloomy day.
Cause the sun chose to stay away.

So it does look like it's going to rain.
Maybe if it does it will wash away my pain.

The clouds are a much darker grey.
Now that the pain won't go away.

I hope tomorrow the sun will shine.
And maybe my pain will be on the decline.

Go

Go away, go away, go away.
Cause in my heart you cannot stay.

Bye, bye- bye.
All you do is lie.

Leave, leave, leave.
You I still can't believe.

Hey, hey, hey.
Please just go away.

Good morning day

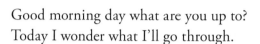

Good morning day what are you up to?
Today I wonder what I'll go through.

I wonder what this new day will be.
And will it be a good day for me.

Good morning day what will you be?
Will you be a good day for me?

Will you be a day of rainbows and butterflies?
Will you be a day they'll be joy in my eyes?

Good morning day what will you be?
I hope you'll be a good day for me.

How many times?

How many times can true love find you?
And find you with a love that's true.

How many times can someone love you?
And love you with a love that's honest and true.

How many times can true love find you?
And how many times would it be true?

How many times can true love find you?
And will love be your dream come true?

How many times can true love find you?
And how many times can love be true?

Hush

You need to learn how to hush.
Cause all you ever sound like is a lush.

You see you do talk too much.
That's why with you I don't keep in touch.

You know you're always saying the wrong thing.
And your words they do seem to sting.

You never have anything good to say.
That's why I try to stay out of your way.

You really should learn how to just hush.
Cause all your words they do seem to crush.

I mean you really do just talk too much.
And that's why I won't keep in touch.

You see all your words do cause a bad smutch.
I can't say anything other than you talk to dang much.

Imagine a world

Imagine a world where there was no pain.
Imagine a world where everyone was sane.

Imagine a world where that could be true.
That's a world someone could get used too.

Now imagine the real world where people often feel blue.
And then imagine pain was the feeling they only knew.

Now imagine that being the reality of my world.
And this was my reality since I was a little girl.

Imagine me having to live and exist in that world.
Imagine, imagine me being that little girl.

Now you're questioning why I am not sane.
It's because my world was so full of pain.

Imagine

Imagine yourself in my world.
Then imagine yourself as me the little girl.

The little girl who felt lost and alone.
The little girl from no one love had been shown.

The little girl that no one truly knew.
The little girl whose world was often time blue.

The little girl who wished she knew love.
The little girl who so often prayed to God above.

The little girl who prayed cause her life was a disaster.
The little girl who only wished that love she could master.

The little girl who was always sad and felt unloved in her heart.
The little girl who felt this way each day her day would start.

The little girl who always in life wished that she knew love.
The little girl who never stopped praying for love from God above.

The little girl who prayed for God to one day answer her prayer.
The little girl who looked up and one day in her life love was there.

The little girl who now knows she has found an honest love.
The little girl whose knows for sure she's loved by God above.

It made me cry

I read one of my poems, and it made me cry.
It was about the little girl whose pain she had to hide.

I felt so sad as I read about her life's pain.
I thought to myself, how is this little girl sane.

I read about her life, and it touched my heart.
I wondered about the little girl as I read from the start.

I thought to myself, how did she grow up so sad.
As I read her story, it made me feel so bad.

I wondered whatever happened to this little girl.
Then I realized I was the little girl, and that was my world.

Lessons on love

Where has the time gone I looked up and now I'm grown.
Grown to face the world and live life with it's unknown.

To make choices for my life when no love was I shown.
I have to show the world the love I haven't known.

Cause now I've grown up and I am someone mother.
And now I have to teach my kids to show love to one another.

How do I teach them something that was never taught to me?
How do I teach them how to love when love I didn't see?

I have to teach them love so they can teach someone else.
But how do I teach them love when I had to teach myself.

I want my kids to grow up with love in their heart.
I want them to know I loved them from the moment their life did start.

I want my kid to take heed from the lessons I taught each one.
And know I taught them well when it's all said and done.

Little girls

There were these little girls who looked up to their mother.
Cause this mother's love was like no other.

She taught them how to be good girls.
And how to navigate through this big ole world.

She taught them how to be nice and polite.
And how between them not to fuss or fight.

She taught them well the things they should know.
Then off to college, each of them would go.

She's always been to them an outstanding mother.
Cause with this mother's love she's like no other.

She has to be so very proud of herself.
Cause she's now doing it with no one's help.

She has to know she stands high above the others.
She has to know she is the world's greatest of mothers.

Little girl lost

Little girl lost who didn't have a father.
Because with her, he couldn't bother.

He left her when she was only four years old.
The reason he left her she's never been told.

For years and years, she always wondered why.
Can you imagine all the tears she did cry?

Now he wants to be bothered because he's dying and old.
Now she doesn't care and could care less if she'll ever be told.

Living with pain

The pain of my heart keeps tearing at my soul.
It keeps reminding me that my heart has a hole.

There's a pain in me that my heart cannot hide.
Sometimes I feel like my heart has died.

I often look at my life in utter and total disgust.
Cause my heart, I cannot and will not ever trust.

There's a pain in my heart that I so often can't bear.
Cause it feels like for me, I can trust no one to be there.

I often wonder how I can live with all this pain.
And here on this earth I somehow choose to remain.

So I guess I'll keep living my life with all of this pain.
But while living this painful life, I have no happiness to gain.

This pain I feel I'll keep hidden way deep inside.
This pain is something I'll always keep trying to hide

I will somehow not let this pain get the best of me.
Cause I'll keep on living and somehow this pain will set me free.

Losing myself

In this relationship, I lost myself.
I truly became someone else.

I didn't know the person I'd become.
I was a person who had become numb.

You see, I had lost myself along the way.
I can't begin to tell you what day.

I remember waking up and asking who, are you?
Cause you have changed into someone new.

I didn't quite understand why I had changed.
But I know my thoughts had become rearranged.

Then I asked myself to find the real me.
So now the real me you once again see.

So I will not ever again lose myself.
Cause I will never change for someone else.

Mask

What's wrong with your life I must ask?
Cause I see you're hiding behind that mask.

Why must you hide the real you from me?
Why don't you want the real you for me to see?

Someday you're going to have to take off that mask.
And in your life, you're going to have to bask.

Don't you know you will have to show the real you?
Even if in this life you don't want too.

So you might as well take off that mask.
Without me telling you it's not a hard task.

So come on and let the real you show.
Cause who you are I really would like to know.

Maybe

I want to be someone's forever lady.
Not a man's just simply maybe.

I want not to always be a man's friend.
And not to be thought of as his kin.

I want to be in a man's heart.
And in his, heart I don't want to depart.

I want to be to a man his one true love.
And when he holds my hand, I fit like a glove.

I want to be a man's one and only wife.
And to be with him for the rest of his life.

I want to be with a man who will love me.
And in his heart, I'll forever and always be.

Me

I cannot be who you want me to be.
Who I am is who you see.

I cannot live by what you say.
I have to live my life my way.

I cannot be who you want me to be.
I have to live my life being me.

So if you can accept me for just who I be.
Who I truly am you truly will see.

Mountains

I see a lot of you in me.
That's why I won't let you be.

I know that you have the spirit to fight.
So I know that you can see clearly, what's right.

You see you have wisdom and you have good insight.
And you have the determination to do what is right.

So as you move forward on this day in time.
Remember, there will always be mountains to climb.

My friend my kin

I have this friend Debra who is as crazy as can be.
When I tell you about this girl this, you will see.

See, when I became a grown-up, we hung out really tough.
But one thing I liked about Debra she was too much.

She had a sense of humor, and boy could she make you laugh.
And boy she was boisterous and would speak on anyone's behalf.

Sometimes she'd even speak loudly and put on a good show.
I'm telling you she was hilarious, and this everyone did know.

I'm telling you this girl was a little bit crazy and a character fo sho.
I'm telling you she always a joy, so our friendship did truly grow.

This girl turned out to be my craziest friend.
That's why I don't look at her as my friend but my kin.

My friend

Are you really, my friend?
So will you be there in the end?

Can I count on you?
With everything I am going through.

Will you be here for me?
Or will I have to wait and see?

Can I call you when I need a friend?
And can I truly count on you in the end?

New chapter

I don't know what this new chapter of my life will bring.
Well, I sure hope it will bring with it a new thing.

I hope that it will bring peace, love, and happiness.
And I hope it won't be filled with more emptiness.

I hope this chapter of my life will be the best.
So in my life I can get that much-needed rest.

Nice

You inspired me to be my best.
You also told me I must take time to rest.

You told me I could do things on my own.
And you showed me I am never alone.

You told me in life to always be strong.
And not to worry when things go wrong.

You gave me so much sound advice.
Thank you so much for being so nice.

Not in vain

I woke up this morning feeling sad and blue.
So I got on my knees and prayed because I had too.

I asked the Lord to take away my pain.
And I hoped my prayer was not in vain.

I asked the Lord to take the pain out of my heart.
And this was what I prayed for from my prayers start.

I knew that I needed the Lord's help.
Cause I couldn't remove it by myself.

I knew that my pain was cutting deep at my soul.
And my pain felt as dark as coal.

So I prayed a prayer that was strong and bold.
And then I waited and here is what I was told.

My child, my child I feel your pain.
So I've taken it away so in your heart it can't remain.

I'm here for you whenever you're feeling blue.
I'm here for you no matter what you're going through.

So when you need me please send up a prayer.
And know when you pray I'll always be there.

One day at a time

I'm living my life one day at a time cause this makes sense to me.
I've found out living life at my own pace truly is the key.

I can't move around living my life at everyone else's pace.
If I did then I would only be running everyone else's race.

I have to live my life on my terms and living it just for me.
Cause I can't always do things everyone else's way this I just can't see.

Cause I cannot live my life living up to everyone else's expectations.
Cause doing things everyone else's way won't give me sweet sensations.

I'm not saying when someone gives me advice I'll turn a deaf ear.
But I want everyone to know their words I truly and honestly hear.

I know I'll have to climb mountains until I reach the top.
I'm going to continue climbing mountains cause this will never stop.

So as I live my life one day at a time and keep doing my best.
I'll always do my best but sometimes I will need time to rest.

So living my life as I see fit is truly in God's plan.
I hope that me, living my life my way, you'll come to understand.

Oops

I cannot speak about your life today.
Cause I have nothing good to say.

I cannot speak with words that are kind.
Cause you are not acting like you have a sound mind.

You are making decisions that I don't quite understand.
And I don't think you are doing the best that you can.

Oops, I said I wouldn't speak on your life today.
But I did cause I had that one thing to say.

So I'll now keep my words and won't say anything else.
Cause I'm putting my feelings high upon the shelf.

Plan

Hey can someone help me to find my Mr. Right?
Cause with the choices I, made I don't have good insight.

You see, I always chose a man that wasn't right for me.
Sometimes that was even so very obvious to see.

But I most often many times turned my little head
And believed and trusted every word a man said.

I know, I know I wasn't very smart.
Cause I saw the warning signs from the start.

But I have a bad habit of looking the other way.
I don't know why I trust and believe every word they say.

So can someone help me to choose a much better man?
And one who's not living his life with a master plan.

Pretty thing

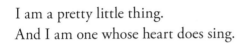

I am a pretty little thing.
And I am one whose heart does sing.

It sings of joy and happiness.
It sings cause I am fabulous.

It sings because I am who I'm meant to be.
And of how beautiful I am for being me.

It sings because I am who I want to be.
My heart sings from the joy of just being me.

Rare

You are the answer to my deepest prayer.
Cause you are someone who's always been there.

You've shown me you truly do care.
And this is something so often time rare.

I'm so thankful for you always being there.
Thank you so much for showing me you care.

And if you ever need me, I'll be there.
To show you for you I also do care.

I want you to know our friendship is rare.
Cause you've always been there in times of despair.

I like to thank you again for always being there.
Thank you again for your love and care.

Righteous

The prayers of the righteous prevails much.
So it's no wonder why my heart you touch.

You see, it's you I come to when I need prayer.
Because I know for me you do care.

You see, I don't just ask for anyone's prayer.
Cause I need someone righteous to be there.

You see, I've watched your relationship with God.
And I know God winks at you and gives you a nod.

So I know when you pray and send up a prayer.
I know for sure God will honor it and be there.

So I'm thanking you for being so righteous and just.
Thank you for your prayers that I can always trust.

Rise and fall

This pain can be the rise and the fall of me.
Will I be from this pain ever set free?

Will this pain always get the best of me?
Once again, from this pain, I must be set free.

The rise of the pain stands at an all-time high.
Sometimes I ask myself, and I wonder why.

Why is this pain at an all-time high?
Why is this pain here with a feeling I can't deny?

The fall of the pain takes me to a place where I feel low.
It takes me to a place that I don't even know.

Why must this pain be the rise and the fall of me?
And from this pain, will I ever be set free?

One day I will set myself free from this pain.
And I'll cry no more tears that fall like winters rain.

Road

Where are you going on this road you are traveling too?
Cause your uncertainty about life is clearly showing its clue.

Why don't you have a clue about where you are going?
Cause your uncertainty about life clearly is showing.

Why do you travel a road in which you've lost your way?
Don't you know on this lost road you cannot stay?

Why must you keep traveling on this road lost?
Don't you know it is you who'll pay the cost?

Scar

You'll have to see my life from a distance.
And this wouldn't be met with resistance.

So away from you, I need to go far.
Cause you left on my heart a scar.

A scar that will take time to heal.
You left a scar that is painful and real.

So away from you, I must go far.
To erase from me this painful scar.

Secret

What are you running from little, girl?
Is there a secret you're hiding from the world?

What don't you want the world to know?
Are you afraid to let your secret show?

Is it something you cannot face?
Cause it seems like you're running in place?

Why can't you share your secret with the world?
What are you hiding from us, little girl?

I'm sure it's nothing and it's probably no big deal.
What are you hiding behind your heart's shield?

Is it so bad that on it you can't speak?
Why can't you share the secret we seek?

Why must we run blindsided alongside you?
Is it something for you we can do?

What are you hiding from us, little girl?
What is this secret you're hiding from the world?

Sometimes

Sometimes I wonder what makes me, me.
Sometimes I wonder if the true me you see.

Sometimes I wonder just who I am.
Sometimes I wonder if you're looking at a scam.

Sometimes I wonder who can I be?
Sometimes I wonder who do you see?

Sometimes I wonder if I'm a star.
Sometimes I wonder if I stand out from afar.

Sometimes I wonder just who can I be.
Sometimes I wonder if it's me that you see.

Sudden

I'm leaning on the everlasting cross.
To help me through this sudden loss.

I never expected you to leave this way.
So it made my heart sad today.

I thought you would always be here.
So it's so sad not to have you near.

I don't know why you had to leave so fast.
But my love for you will forever last.

I'm going to miss you so very much.
Cause my heart you've always seemed to touch.

I don't know when, I've ever been this sad.
I just know my heart feels bad.

I'm going to miss you this I truly know.
But while you were here, my love for you did show.

I'll always wonder why you had to leave so fast.
Cause you'll never be to me just a memory of my past.

And as I wonder why you had to go that way.
I'll keep loving you every single day.

Tell me something

Tell me something about you I don't know.
Cause what I know about you seems to show.

I know that you are always loving and kind.
And when it comes to helping, me you never mind.

So tell me something about you, I don't know.
I'll tell you this your kind heart does show.

Thank you

Thank you for being here for me.
In my heart, you will always be.

I thank you for being so loving and kind.
For this reason, you stay on my mind.

I couldn't have asked God for a better friend.
So words of gratitude from my heart I now send.

So no matter which way our friendship works out.
Your heart and friendship, I'll never doubt.

Again thank you again for being here for me.
So forever in my heart you'll always be.

The devil's name was Sharon

Here's another of my life stories and what did in it unfold.
And its about more secret of my life and the pain my life does hold.

It's about a little girl whose bigger sister who would always fight her.
It will be in full detail of my life and what really did occur.

This sister used to only fight two sisters why we never knew.
So beating me and my sister up was all she used to do.

I never understood why she beat me up, and my mother would do
nothing.
I as, being a little girl, wanted my mother to step in and just do
something.

It often seemed to me her beating had no consequence.
And to make things a little worse, these beating just didn't make any
sense.

I never could escape the wrath of this devil of which we called Sharon.
This other sister she used to beat up her name was like hers, just Kharon.

I never had enough courage to try to fight her back.
If I did I knew only a more vengeful Sharon would attack.

I tried so many times when she was angry to stay out of her way.
But she was angry all the time, so it didn't matter what the day.

She beat me up way into my teenage years.
So often when I seen she was mad my heart just filled with fear.

This devil I call Sharon truly was a smart girl.
But I didn't understand why anger filled her world.

I was so glad when she moved out and went off to college.
Cause Sharon was so truly smart she had a lot of book knowledge.

The beating only stopped because Sharon had moved away.
I asked my mother why she didn't do something and scared of her was all that she would say.

But when Sharon returned home she was a changed person.
I guess cause she grew up and was filled with a new emotion.

Them I asked her one day why she fought me so much.
I guess to that question her heart it seemed to touch.

And her answer to me was I blamed you for daddy going away.
I told her I was only four years old when that man chose not to stay.

So all those years I was getting beat up was for the decisions of that man.
That's just one more reason why the man she calls daddy I cannot stand.

Through

I'm thinking of you at this point in time.
Because what he did to you, I feel it is a crime.

He stole your heart and then ran away.
Now because of him, your heart's gone astray.

He left you in a place of pain in which your heart can't bear.
Now your heart finds itself in total disrepair.

He fooled us all with the way he did act.
Cause we thought he had wisdom and tact.

I know he left you with much pain and heartache.
But he'll find out one day he made a mistake.

And he'll come running back like men always do.
But it will be you to say no, with you I am through.

Trouble

Trouble has seemed to come my way.
Why is it so bothersome today?

Why has trouble chosen me?
And why won't trouble just let me be?

I didn't ask for trouble to come my way.
So I hope it's not here to stay.

This trouble has me feeling all alone,
I'll be glad when this trouble has gone.

Why oh why has trouble chosen me?
I wish that trouble would just let me be.

True colors

Why do you care that they were talking about you?
When you know what they've said is so untrue.

Is it because they talked about you with such and such?
You already know they all talk to dang much.

Don't worry about that you've got enough on your plate.
You know what they said you cannot relate.

Please don't get yourself all worked up because of what they've said.
Don't let their untrue words play games with your head.

You know there just talking because there jealous of you.
And they are people who got nothing better to do.

So again, don't worry about them talking to such and such.
Cause they'll always be jealous so they'll always talk too much.

And besides, they are showing you they were never truly your friend,
I say that because they've shown their true colors in the end.

True happiness

Get up, get up, get up, get up.
You got too much self-pity in your cup.

Why are you always feeling down on your luck?
I'm telling you you're doing things to make your life suck.

You have to do things in a different way.
Then it will make for a much better day.

So get up, get up, get up, get up.
And let happiness fill your cup.

So again, get up, get up, get up, get up.
And let life's true happiness finally develop.

Ugly inside

Some people are downright real mean and ugly inside.
There so mean and ugly their true feelings they can't hide

Some people never have anything nice or kind words to say.
Some people are mean, hateful and downright ugly every day.

I don't know why some people are simply that way.
I guess love never made it in their hearts to stay.

Those kinds of people you need to keep out of your life.
Cause their hearts are only filled with envy and strife.

Those kinds of people don't make for a good friend.
If you stay around them, you'll be like them in the end.

So you can't be around people who are simply like that.
Cause if you do in the end that's where your heart will be at.

Wandering

I'm wandering around in darkness cause I cannot see.
But I want to know is this darkness what's inside of me.

This darkness has a way of hiding its bright light.
I can't see what hides cause it hides as if it's night.

I wonder what's in this darkness for I cannot see what's there.
Is the darkness only in my mind because my mind it seems to scare.

I know this darkness seem to follow me wherever I may go.
I think I'd like to see what this darkness does not seem to show.

What's there wandering along side of me that follows wherever I go.
Is this darkness something that my mind will come to know?

Why am I always wandering around in darkness where I cannot see?
Or is this darkness in my mind the darkness that's just inside of me.

We are here for you

Talking to you makes us happy and sad.
To hear what you went through with our dad.

We're so sorry for the experiences that you went through.
If we had known we would have helped you.

No child deserves to be treated that way.
Is all with our hearts we can truly say.

We wish that we had all knew.
It's no way we wouldn't have sent for you.

We wouldn't have allowed for you to be treated that way.
We would all have rallied around you to save your day.

Our hearts really and truly goes out to you.
Because of all that you have gone through.

We're so glad that you got away from all that mess.
Cause how he treated you he'll never confess.

We are all happy to hear now that you are doing o.k.
We want you to know we'll be here for you in every way.

Welcome

We welcome you to our family.
Now you can add us to your family tree.

We will all show you the love you miss.
And fill your heart with love and bliss.

We want you to know we are all here for you.
To fill your heart with a love that's true.

So welcome, welcome to the family.
Now the branches spread wide on your family tree.

What I say

You may not want to hear what I say.
I'll speak the truth to you today.

I may speak whatever comes to mind.
Sometimes it may not be so kind.

Sometimes it will be neither right nor wrong.
Sometimes I'll say it in my heart's song.

But no matter what, I'll have to say.
I hope for sure it brightens up your day.

Where this goes

I don't know where this may go.
I wonder if you even know.

What is this ever going to be?
Is there something special between you and me?

If what happens turns out nice.
To your life, I will add spice.

But if life throws us a curveball.
Together victorious we'll still stand tall.

But if you become only my friend.
I still will love you till the end.

Where your heart's at

That man from your past should just stay there.
Cause with other women with him you did share.

It's a reason for why that relationship didn't last.
That's why he should be that just a memory of your past.

Why you left him is no great mystery.
The reason you left him was so plain to see.

Now your entertaining the thought of now taking him back.
Why is it, is it some misery in your life you now lack?

Why would you consider being with him again?
Why when he wasn't a good man or even a good friend.

He's the only one who'll benefit from that.
Girl, is that really where your heart's at?

Girl, I'm talking to you, you don't need to take him back.
Are you sure in your life it's not pain that you lack?

Can't you see with him you'll have nothing to gain?
Considering taking him back would surely be insane.

Girl, I thought you were so much smarter than that.
Cause with him I know that's not where your heart can be at.

Who are you?

Who are you, the person standing before me?
Are you the person I truly do see?

Are you a person that shows the true you?
Or are you the person I already knew?

Who are you, the person that I see?
Who are you, truly the person that's standing before me?

Who are you, the person I really want to know?
Who are you, the person whose beauty does show?

Who are you, the person that I see?
Who are you, the person that's staring back at me?

Why must you cry?

Why must you cry, why do you cry little girl?
Are there things that make you sad in your world?

Why must you cry, are you truly that sad?
Why can't you think of ways to make you feel glad?

Why do you feel so sad I want to know?
Cause I see you crying, so your sadness does show.

I can't help your heart to heal if you don't tell me why.
I need to know why all the tears you do cry.

So stop crying and tell me why your heart is so sad.
Then I'll help you to find a way to make your heart glad.

Wish

I wished upon a falling star.
My wish was that you weren't so far.

Another wish was that you were here.
Cause yet you're so far when I want you near.

Yet you are many miles away.
I still think of you every day.

I want you here cause you are just too far.
I guess I'll have to keep wishing on a star.

So it can bring you close to me.
Cause it is you, I want to see.

Woman

I am a woman who heart you've did harm.
I am a woman you've finessed with your charm.

I am a woman who stuck by you with your mess.
I am a woman who you didn't treat your best.

I am a woman who cried many of tears.
I am a woman who stuck by you for years.

I am a woman who you didn't appreciate.
I am a woman in which you didn't relate.

I am a woman who has now chosen to walk away.
I am a woman who doesn't believe a word that you say.

I am a woman who has to make her own way.
I am a woman that in her heart you can't stay.

I am a woman who has now set you free.
I am a woman who now learned to love me.

World

Out of nowhere here came you.
Ready to introduce to my world something new.

Something new to a world full of pain.
Introducing me to the happiness, that shall rain.

A world now filled with promise and hope.
And with this new world I can now cope.

A world no longer sad or blue.
And it is all because of you.

Relationship

Abuse

All the abuse you put me through.
Was something I had gotten used too.

I forgot how to be treated right.
I didn't know just how to fight.

No, I wasn't physically abused.
But no doubt I was being used.

I stayed there accepting all of your mess.
And I didn't realize you weren't treating me the best.

I accepted this for many, many years.
And I can't begin to count all my tears.

I put up with so much mess from you.
It's no wonder that we are now through.

And it's because of all the things you did do.
I still loved you with my love which was true.

But from you your love wasn't the same.
So the love in my heart didn't remain.

But I'll say I never wanted to break up.
But I had to because I had, had enough.

Now I'm use to you being out of my life.
So now you can stop asking me to be your wife.

So I guess for now you can only be my friend.
Cause my heart needs time to mend.

Adore

I want a chance to get to know you.
Cause this is something I'd like to do.

I can't seem to get you off my mind.
I think you are a man who is one of a kind.

Cause you truly do make my heart soar.
You are the man I've come to adore.

Apart

You left me and the days of my world fell apart.
And I didn't know how each day would start.

I didn't know which way I should go.
I tell you I just didn't know.

I was so lost and often time confused.
I walked around thinking what else would I lose.

I didn't know just where to begin.
I only knew for sure I'd lost my friend.

I didn't know just what to think.
I sometimes felt like I would sink.

I knew that I had to change my ways.
Or I was in for more bad days.

I had to kneel down and begin to pray.
For God to take my pain and sadness away.

I believed God would do this for me.
And now I have a clear vision to see.

I'm starting my life now over again.
And I can see why we aren't to each other a friend.

Sometimes we have to change things up a bit.
So now I accept between us our split.

I'll see you from now on for who you are.
But I'll see you this way from afar.

I no longer see you as the man for me.
And in my life from now on you won't be.

So let me now say goodbye.
So tears for you I'll no longer cry.

So my days won't be spent thinking of you.
Cause you are not my dream come true.

Beautiful love

My heart is open to finding what could be love.
Something so pure as a beautiful white dove.

A love that gets better and better as time goes by.
A love so beautiful my heart cannot deny.

A love that will make all my dreams come true.
A love that's designed by God that's new.

Believe

I wear my heart upon my sleeve.
Because in love I do believe.

I want a love, that's pure and divine.
A love that I can truly call mine.

I want a love that is right for me.
Cause in my heart loved they'll always be.

I want a love that will never end.
And a love that will be my friend.

Boyfriend

You keep saying you were a good boyfriend.
But you broke my heart, and it didn't mend.

I keep wondering why you keep saying that.
Cause I know in your, heart I was not at.

You say that because you were often time nice.
And to my life, you did add some spice.

But you were a man I couldn't trust.
And you had an image that was so robust.

How you've convinced yourself that you were a good man.
This I truly cannot see or even begin to understand.

You see for me you weren't your best you.
And you know this is something so very true.

So the next time you say to me you were a good man.
Explain it to me clearly so I can understand.

Brings me fear

♥

Where do we both go from here?
Cause being with you again brings me fear.

I don't know if I can trust you.
Cause of the things you did do.

You showed me I couldn't trust you with my heart.
So I don't know if we can have a new start.

I don't' think about giving you a second chance.
I don't even look your way and even glance.

Cause there were many things you shouldn't have done.
I don't know then why I didn't just run.

Now you want me to be with you again.
Why should I do that when you weren't my friend?

Clown

My feelings for you are fading.
Cause to me, you've been degrading.

You are always saying things to put me down.
And then you laugh at me as if I'm a clown.

You are not always really nice to me.
So in your heart, I just can't be.

I guess it's time for me to walk away.
So I'm moving on with my life today.

Don't want you back

When did you decide you wanted me back?
Cause now you're trying to tell me that's where your heart's at.

I can't believe now that you truly want me.
Cause your wanting me is something I just can't see.

I tried for months and months to get you to take me back.
But you didn't want me, and I was as serious as a heart attack.

I cried so many tears cause you didn't want me.
Now you're trying to tell me it's me you now see.

I remember how you kept pushing me aside.
Now you're telling me you want me, and I tell you you're a lie.

I wanted so very badly for you to love me again.
I'm telling you I was heartbroken, and my heart wouldn't mend.

I told you I loved you, but you only wanted to be my friend.
I was trying to save our relationship so it wouldn't have to end.

Now I'm in a place where my heart can't forgive you.
Because I often told you just what not to do.

Now I don't know the answer to the problem you're facing.
Cause I think about us being together is a dream you are now chasing.

Cause sometimes you can break someone's heart beyond repair.
I have to tell you now that's a place in my heart in which I am there.

I would advise you to move on and find yourself someone else.
Cause my love for you has been moved and put high up on a shelf.

Right now, I will not cause I cannot see myself being with you again.
So I think it will be best if you just accept me as a friend.

Dream

My dream can come true I know it can.
The dream I dream of you being my man.

A dream that will turn my world from grey.
And a dream of having the sunshine every day.

The dream I've had cause you're a good man.
A dream that maybe even part of your plan.

You see, I hope my dream you'll understand.
Of how much I dream of you being my man.

Dreaming if you

I wake up each morning after dreaming of you.
Tossed and turned the whole night is all I could do.

I woke up this morning feeling kind of strange.
And wonder why these bad dreams I can't seem to change.

My dreams are always hard and uncomfortable to bear.
I can't help but wonder why you are always a nightmare.

I don't like having dreams, dreams that are of you.
So falling to sleep is something I don't like to do.

One day maybe soon, you'll be out of my dream.
And the sound of pure joy in my dreams I will scream.

Falling

I find myself falling and falling for you.
What in the world should I do?

Should I make a stand or just run away?
Should I run from you the man who makes my day?

Cause you are a man who is gentle and kind.
You are a man who stays so heavy on my mind.

That's why I find myself falling and falling for you.
So will you be the man whose love will be true?

Fuzzy feelings

I get warm and fuzzy feelings when I think of you.
Cause I'm thinking about a love so genuine and true.

A love that I can relax and enjoy.
Cause I'll be with a man who is not a boy.

A man whose specialty is to love.
Cause he has learned from God above.

And a man who will stand there by my side.
And a man who will stand there proudly with pride.

Gained a friend

I have a sense of happiness since you have been around.
No longer holding on to anger and strife am I bound.

But I surely don't know where this may go.
But a true friend in me will always show.

I may not end up being your wife.
But you have gained a friend for life.

Getting things straight

First of all, let's get things straight.
You are in no way my soulmate.

You broke my heart and walked away.
I was very sad that day.

You left me, and my heart was blue.
And there was nothing I could do.

I wanted you here at home with me.
But this was something you couldn't see.

You left me with a mind confused.
No way did I think it was you I'd lose.

The pain I wake up with brings me sorrow.
And now I don't see happiness in my tomorrow.

You've hurt me and my heart's full of pain.
In doing this what in the world did you gain?

Good find

I met a man who was one of a kind
And I'm telling you he was a good find.

He only had nice things to say.
So that's why he made my day.

I'm telling you this man was so nice.
And to my life, he did add some spice.

So I was sad when he went away.
Because I really wanted him to stay.

I have not yet gotten over him.
That's why today my light is now dim.

Goodbye

I was not ready to say goodbye.
I tell you this is not a lie.

I tried so hard to simply tell you.
But this you would not listen too.

I cried for many days and sometimes night.
And the tears were because you left my sight.

I was sad and often time blue.
I found myself not knowing what to do.

I laid there crying in my bed.
Cause you would not listen to a word, I said.

I tried so hard to convince you.
That there was no reason for us to be through.

But you just turned a deaf ear.
And your leaving was the sum of my fear.

I never saw you leaving my sight.
So when you left it didn't seem right.

I waited and waited for you to return
But you didn't and you showed no concern.

You made up your mind, and this was the end.
So I lost the person I wanted as my friend.

I guess I have to accept things for what they are.
And I guess I'll have to love you from afar.

Harm

I am angry about how you left that day.
To utter a word about your leaving nothing did you say.

So your leaving came as one big surprise.
So my sadness I just could not hide.

I never saw a sign that you were leaving that day.
You snuck out and moved away.

I know you knew that would hurt me.
But hurting me was something you couldn't see.

I cried so much cause you were gone.
You'll never know to my heart the harm.

It took me a while to recover from it.
Now in my life, you do not fit.

You chose to move away and hurt my heart.
Now I have to have a brand new start.

I thought I'd never get over you.
But this was something I had to do.

So no more tears must I have to cry.
Cause you didn't want me and this you can't deny.

I'll always remember the pain you did cause.
So now I know your love has flaws.

Heartbeat

I met you, and at once, I knew.
That you are a good man, and this is so true.

I knew you were the guy for me.
And this to me was plain to see.

So it came as no surprise.
That thoughts of you made my temperature rise.

I was hoping that you would see what I see.
That I thought you and I was meant to be.

So I wanted you to stay for a while.
Because you did make my heart smile.

That's why I was sad when you walked away.
Cause not a word of your leaving did you say.

I wanted you to stay, so your leaving did hurt me.
But the pain from your leaving me you didn't see.

I haven't quite yet gotten over you.
I guess because I didn't want us to be through.

But I will need a little more time.
To finally accept that you are not mine.

Hear the words

Did you hear the words I don't love you?
And it's all because of what you've put me through.

You put me through a lot of mess.
My life with you was so full of stress.

You were to me, not a good man.
So I put you out of my life I had to take a stand.

Cause being with you won't work for me anymore.
Cause for me you, I no longer adore.

You've done things to show me who you are.
And you left on my life a big ole scar.

I'm so good, just being without you.
Cause you're not in my life to put me through.

So I'm repeating it I'm through with you.
So leave me alone because there's nothing more you can do.

Heart no key

To my heart, you no longer have a key.
I hope this is something you can now see.

You are gone, and now I'm free.
Cause in my heart you'll never be.

You left me, and my heart shouts hooray.
Cause I know my worlds filled with a better day.

I thought when you left my heart had died.
From all those millions of tears I cried.

I couldn't imagine life without you.
Cause I thought you were my dream come true.

Now that you've gone, my life has gotten better.
And it's all because we are no longer together.

Hooray

I saw you yesterday.
And my heart shouted hooray.

You made my heart skip a beat.
Seeing you was like a sweet treat.

You don't know what you do to me.
My day brightens up when you I see.

I know when I see you my heart fills with joy.
And all I think is boy, oh boy.

I want you to know you are one of a kind.
And I can never seem to get you off my mind.

I hope you will be a life- long friend.
And I hope together we will be in the end.

Hope

I saw you the other day.
And it seemed like you were o.k.

I even thought I saw you smile.
If I say I don't miss you, then I'll be in denial.

I don't know why this made my heartache.
But your leaving I know was a mistake.

I sometimes fantasize about being with you again.
But I know your heart won't bend.

I hope I run into you again.
Cause I hope you'll be my friend in the end.

I am here

I am here for you, as you are here for me.
What will become of us what will this friendship be?

I'm at a place in time where I want and need to know.
Cause these feeling I have for you truly must show.

I want to be more then just your friend.
Cause I'm the woman on whom you can depend.

I'd like to walk together with you on this road we call life.
And show you if you choose me I'd make you a good wife.

I am a woman

I may not be the kind of woman you are use too.
But I am a woman whose love is true.

I am a woman that's most of the times nice.
I am a woman whose love is precise.

I am a woman who would make you a good wife.
I am a woman who'll bring joy to your life.

I am a woman who can be called strong.
I am a woman who won't do your heart wrong.

I am a woman who is rare.
I am a woman who will always be there.

I am a woman who will listen when you talk.
I am a woman who'll hold your hand as you walk.

I am a woman on whom you can depend.
I am a woman who will be to you a good friend.

I can

I can love you I know I can.
Because I see you are a good man.

I see a man who's faithful and true.
And for love, its nothing he won't do.

I know I can love you I know I can.
Because I see you are really a good man.

I don't want you

Why do you want me now when I don't want you?
I cried and cried because of all you put me through.

Now that I've moved on which is my right.
Now you want to rally around me and put up a fight.

I truly don't want you is all I can say.
So stay out of my life now and have a good day.

I loved you

Why I love you I don't know.
I guess my heart just told me so.

I guess I looked away as I often did.
And tried to ignore the secrets you hid.

I often looked away cause I didn't want to see.
All the wrong things you were doing to me.

I kept the blinders on my eyes as I looked away.
Cause in my heart, I loved you and wanted you to stay.

I thought you were going to be the greatest man.
And I stood up for you and said oh him you don't understand.

I often told myself you could honestly be to me a better man.
And I told myself, girl, stand up for your heart and take a better stand.

And to take care of yourself cause you deserve so much better.
But I'm so used to being treated bad so it to me didn't matter.

I guess when you only know pain you accept being treated that way.
But I know it's time for me to stand up and make myself a better day.

If I never see you

If I never see you again.
I'll always think of you as a friend.

I won't think of you as a man who's not kind.
I'll think maybe you just had a lot on your mind.

I won't think anything bad or have bad thoughts about you.
Even though how you think of me may not be true.

I'll always think good thoughts of you.
And of how I thought you were my dream come true.

I'll think thoughts of how I still wish you were mine.
Cause thoughts of you, my mind and heart can't decline.

Cause you see, you left such an impression on my heart.
And I thought you were going to be my new start.

I guess I was just wrong, and it wasn't meant to be.
But you know the heart, see's what it just wants to see.

It ain't about me

I can write you a story that you'll think It's about my life.
And how I wanted to be anybody just somebody's wife.

Then you'll come to understand the poem isn't about me.
You'll laugh, and you'll smile as you realize the poem is about thee.

Cause you see you jump, from one relationship to another.
And I thought in those relationships y'all was in love with each other.

But how many men can you love in one lifetime?
And when I think about those men, they're all just slime.

You see I can't keep up with all the lovers you've had.
And If I mention how many men it's truly just sad.

Please stop excepting those men love cause it's only a Lil bit.
And stop being with men who are just a misfit.

And then tell all those losers your heart's now in bliss.
Cause their Lil bit of love your heart does not miss.

It's about you

My poetry sometimes are inspired by you.
Cause at one time you were my dream come true.

In the beginning you were so nice and kind.
I thought you were a very good find.

But you turned out to be not the man of my dreams.
Cause you so often time pulled so many schemes.

You turned out to be not my mister right.
Cause you done me wrong when you were out of my sight.

I had a hard time believing that you weren't a good man.
But after the first sign of infidelity I should have just ran.

You see you really did me wrong and you put me through so much.
And now you are wondering why my heart you can't touch.

I should have run and run and run a long time ago.
Because of how untrusting of a man you are truly did show.

I've dated him before

I had the same problem, just a different man.
I was in love with someone I couldn't stand.

He did things to me that shouldn't have been done.
He made my life with him, not much fun.

He ran around playing his little game.
He made me feel like I was going insane.

I don't know why I chose to stay.
When I knew I should have told him to go away.

He cheated and lied, he was not a good man.
So from him, I should have run fast as I can.

I don't know why I didn't let him go.
When I knew in my heart, I should have said no.

Now that's he's, gone I don't understand.
Why I chose to stay with that man.

He wasn't a good man for me.
But this was something I couldn't see.

I've dated a man like him before.
And I showed that man the front door.

Why did it take me so long to see?
This man would never be right for me.

Now that he has gone away.
Away from me, I'll let him stay.

Let me tell you

Let me tell you this.
It's you I don't miss.

Let me tell you this.
You, I can dismiss.

Let me tell you this.
My heart is now in bliss.

Lies

I will no longer sit back and listen to your lies.
Cause listening to your lies makes my temperature rise.

Listening to your lies makes my blood curl.
Cause I will not be anymore that naïve girl.

You see, I can now decipher your lie.
So when I talk to you I wonder why.

Why you insist on explaining things to me.
But I can tell when you're lying, so just let me be.

I won't ever again be that once naïve girl.
Cause I now live in a whole different world.

So you don't have to keep telling me lies.
This way my temperature won't be on the up rise.

You see, I will not let your lies mess with my head.
Cause I won't believe a word of which you've said.

So when you talk to me don't tell me a lie.
That way your words I won't have to deny.

But I know when you talk to me you'll continue to lie.
So that's why I'm telling you this simple word good-bye.

Listen

You are not listening.
We are not a couple or a thing.

Why are you not listening to me?
To my heart you no longer have the key.

Cause you were not wise or even smart.
When you simply chose to break my heart.

So now I'll show you with you I am through.
Cause I'm going to find myself someone new.

Cause loving you just wasn't enough for you.
Because you turned out to be someone untrue.

So now, together, I know we are through.
Cause there's nothing more we can do.

So this relationship had to come to an end.
Cause you stop being a true friend.

Little did I know

Little did I know how amazing of a man you are.
I couldn't see this from the distance cause it was just too far.

Since there's no more distance, I can experience my dream.
The dream of having the pleasure of us being a team.

I was not looking for love, so love came as such a surprise.
So I now have the best life cause I have you for my prize.

Lost

I feel so lost and alone without you.
I thought you were my dream come true.

I thought you were a man genuinely kind.
This side of you I now see truly blows my mind.

I put you on a pedal stool that no one could reach.
I thought to me there was so much you'd teach.

I thought I'd found in you the perfect man.
But your sudden exit I don't and can't understand.

Cause you are too old not to express how you feel.
Letting someone know your feeling should be the real.

So the next time you start something new with someone else.
Be sure to reveal to them simply your true self.

Master plan

Why were you ever in my life?
If you knew you couldn't treat me right.

Why would you put yourself there just to bring me pain?
Was it something there for you to gain?

I don't know why you got in this relationship.
Cause this is one someone warned me to skip.

You knew well what kind of man you would be.
A man who lived his life as if he were free.

You could have saved me from heartache and pain.
So there would be no tears I would cry like rain.

I guess you know you are a selfish man.
And a man who lives his life with a master plan.

Matter

It didn't matter that I was there.
To show you so many times that I care.

It didn't matter how I felt.
You didn't acknowledge all my help.

I tried to show I cared for you.
But you didn't care what I would do.

I tried so hard to show you love.
But you pushed me away with a shove.

I couldn't get you to love me right.
So now I'm gone cause I have no fight.

So I only have one thing to say.
I want you to know I loved you in every way.

Missing you

I showered you with love, and you showered me with gifts.
But even with that, we had so many little tiffs.

We tried so hard to get along.
That's why I was shocked when things went wrong.

You had decided you had, had enough.
I didn't know to you things had gotten tough.

Cause you never said a word to me.
So I didn't know you wanted to be free.

Your leaving came as a big surprise.
Your leaving did hurt I tell you no lie.

I never expected you to walk away from me.
But I cried for you every day and this you didn't see.

I want you to know that you are someone I miss.
But I've come to accept you are no longer in bliss.

I think of you often even though you walked away.
Cause I'm going to be missing you every day.

My dream come true

Boy, boy, boy, look at you seem like I found my dream come true.
Cause you are someone special, and I'm just so crazy about you.

You see you are someone different and you are one of a kind.
And you are someone I can't seem to get off of my mind.

I really became a winner and with you I've hit the jackpot.
Cause with other people a winner I was just not.

You see, words can't express how happy from now on I will be.
Cause you are someone who, when I'm with I can be me.

I never thought I would meet someone like you.
Cause you are honestly for me, just my dream come true.

My feelings

Please don't ask my true feelings cause from you I won't hide.
These feelings of frustration has not yet come to subside.

I cannot tell you why this anger hasn't gone away.
I wake up every morning angry, and it stays with me all day.

It's hard trying to convince myself it's not my fault you left that day.
Cause I have come to realize your feelings for me went away.

I have to imagine myself now living my life without you.
I sometimes ask myself, girl, now what are you going to do.

Cause I have spent years and years with you as my man.
I have to believe your leaving was part of God's master plan.

My heart's song

Can I tell you my heart's song?
It's about a love that went so wrong.

It's about the man of which I had dreamed.
But his love was not as it seemed.

His love was wrong and so untrue.
Oh the pain he did put me through.

His love for me was so unreal.
But my heart he'd managed to steal.

But he made my heart sing a sad song.
Cause for my heart he was so wrong.

With everything he put me through.
How wrong for me he was I had no clue.

Then he had the nerve to walk out on me.
Now my heart's song what shall it be.

Nightmare

Look at us things, aren't as good as they seem.
Cause you really are a nightmare from a dream.

You are truly one scary kind of man.
You are someone from whom I should have ran.

I didn't know the nightmare I was going to live.
And with all of that the heartache you'd give.

See you turned out to be my Mister Wrong.
Cause you made my heart fill with a sad song.

You see, I never expected our relationship to be like this.
I thought for sure it would be one of bliss.

But it turned out to be a bad thing.
So you no longer tug at my heart string.

So I guess we both know this is not working.
Because you no longer make my heart sing.

No more pain

The anger of my sadness has now gone away.
I'm just glad in my heart it didn't stay.

So they'll be no more days of pain and sorrow.
But brighter days today and for me tomorrow.

I thought the pain would simply last forever.
Because we would not ever again be together.

But sometimes things aren't what they seem.
Cause I thought you were a man on my team.

But it's ok now cause my life is without you.
I could be happy in life without you who knew.

I'm happy again and that's what life's about.
I can stand up now and hooray I can shout.

I'm so happy in my heart cause I'm doing what's best.
I'm sure happy I have passed life's little rough test.

Not my superstar

How can I ever trust you again?
With that message to my heart you did send.

You once again managed to hurt me.
I know the pain from it you had to see.

But it didn't matter to you.
What I was truly going through.

Now you want me to be with you again.
Why when you weren't to me a good friend.

Now I don't know if I can do that.
Cause that's not where my hearts at.

It took me a while for my heart to heal.
Now my heart you cannot steal.

I see you for who you truly are.
A man that's not my superstar.

I thought you were the man of my dream.
But I now know things weren't as they seem.

It took me a while for me to see.
You weren't the right man for me.

Not your fool

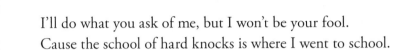

I'll do what you ask of me, but I won't be your fool.
Cause the school of hard knocks is where I went to school.

I let you play games with my feelings for a while.
I even did it while I was wearing a smile.

You thought you had gotten over on me.
But what you done was set me free.

I probably would have left you after a while.
Then we'll see who in the end would be wearing that smile.

Pain

I have no words to say for how you chose to walk away.
I know I still feel the pain of how I felt that day.

A pain that cut so deep it makes me hurt inside.
A pain that cut so deep I cannot seem to hide.

A pain that feels like it will never go away.
A pain that says to my heart that it is here to stay.

Plain to see

I loved you was so plain to see.
So why won't now you just let me be.

I gave to you my whole heart.
What you done to it was not too smart.

I was your girl and I thought you were my friend.
But what you did to my heart made our friendship end.

Now what we had is over so you have to move on with your life.
So please just stop asking me to be your loving wife.

I want to know why now you're trying to be so much more.
Cause you see I've left you alone so my heart can now soar.

So why are you trying when it was you who walked out the door?
Is it because I've left you alone so my heart can now soar?

Prayer

I had to get someone to pray for me when you walked away.
They sent up a powerful prayer to God with the words they did say.

They asked God to take away the sadness that was in my heart.
That was the first thing they said when their prayer for me did start.

You see, I had to ask someone to pray for me cause I needed Gods help.
Cause I couldn't deal with the pain that was in my heart all by myself.

The pain that was there was very painful and often time hard to bear.
The pain that was in my heart was caused by your not being there.

I don't know why I took your leaving so very hard at times to accept.
But often times in my mind and my heart you have always crept.

I say it hasn't gotten any easier to not think so much about you.
Cause often in my quiet moments that is something I can't help but do.

I find myself asking myself do you at any time think of me.
Then I have to tell myself to stop thinking of you and just let things be.

Cause I find myself wanting to pick up the phone to hear your voice.
Then I stop cause I tell myself that would not be a smart choice.

So I have to find some way somehow to let you go.
But how will I do that I honestly and truly do not know.

Prenup

I see that you have falling why won't you pick yourself up?
I told you so many times before you get married to sign a prenup.

Now your marriage is now over and have since fell apart.
I warned you about this person from the beginning of you all start.

I told you this person was not and will not ever be to you a good fit.
And I told you a long time ago that person you should just quit.

You didn't want to listen or take heed to the words that I had said.
Now I hope you'll listen when I tell you to stop lying in that bed.

It's time now to get up and get a move on and go on with your life.
And I hope you'll choose better next time you marry and take on a new wife.

Putting an end

Can I tell you something that you need to know?
I've been through with you some time ago.

I tried to hang on even though no love was there.
Because at one point in time for you, I did care.

I tried telling myself not to leave you alone.
But I knew in my heart the love for you was gone.

I tried holding on for dear life, but I knew we were through.
Because I knew for myself, I wanted to find someone new.

So this is why I have to put an end to this.
So I can find someone who will fill my heart with bliss.

Rain

Didn't you think your leaving would hurt me?
Why was hurting me something you couldn't see?

I know you know that would cause me pain.
And I know you know my tears would fall like rain.

I don't understand how you could be so heartless.
I know you know your leaving caused me to be a mess.

I wondered how it was so easy for you to walk away.
I hope for your life your leaving makes for you a better day.

Same ole me

Every day I talk to you it's the same ole thing.
When I talk to you, no joy to my heart you bring.

I listen to you talk, and talk and my feelings haven't changed.
The feelings in my heart have not yet been rearranged.

I wonder why the feelings of love have not yet returned.
It might be because there are so many things about you I've learned.

I try hard to just forget about the things in our past.
But somehow, I feel my feelings are a result of the aftermath.

I cannot forget about all the wrong things you have done to me.
So that's why when we talk, I only feel just free.

I can't imagine that in your heart now I can truly be.
Cause I'm the same person you left, I'm still the same ole me.

Smart

You put my heart in jeopardy in so many ways.
And you have done this many of days.

You see, you put my heart totally in danger.
Sometimes I was better off trusting it with a stranger.

You did things, and it didn't matter who'd lose.
And I often wonder is someone else I should choose.

You done things in our relationship that just weren't right.
That's why our relationship could never again be alright.

You see, you've done so many bad things that broke my heart.
That's why I walked away from you when I became smart.

Sneak

Your words are always a little bleak.
Cause you are such a sneak.

And no I do not trust you.
And how do you expect me too?

You have not been a trust worthy man.
You live your life with a secret plan.

And you've never been an honest man.
Why I don't know, and I don't understand.

I gave you every single part of me.
But the kind of man you are I couldn't see.

I wonder how I could have been so blind.
To let you get in my heart and mind.

You see you weren't to me a true man.
Cause you lived your life by a dishonest plan.

So this is why I'm telling you I'm letting you go.
So the reasons why I'm leaving you you'll always know.

Space

I haven't written to you today.
It isn't because I had nothing to say.

I just thought I'd give you some space.
And I wanted to put my mind in a different place.

It wasn't because you weren't on my mind.
I thought I'd do something better with my time.

It's because I have to start now letting you go.
And it's because my heart is telling me so.

Maybe one day you'll come to understand.
That I no longer want you as my man.

So now I have to write to you less.
And get myself to a better place, I guess.

So I'm ending my thoughts of you today.
Cause I have nothing more to say.

Special

I met you when you were a young man.
It was then that something special between us began.

I liked you then, so our hearts were bound.
And I always enjoyed when you came around.

Somehow in life, we went our separate ways.
But I tried to find you a many of days.

You see, I have never forgotten about you.
Cause I always thought of you as my dream come true.

Strange

There are so many things that come back to my mind.
Like why were you to me often not kind.

Why did you have to treat me so very bad?
So many times, you made me feel so sad.

What was it that made you not care about me?
I thought to you I was the best I could be.

I really thought I was doing things right.
Because with you I did not even argue or fight.

I held on to hope and that somehow you would change.
But you are someone who is just truly strange.

That's why I can no longer be in this relationship.
Cause you are someone who has on his shoulder a big chip.

Take a stand

You can do better, and I know that you can.
You can do better than that sorry excuse of a man.

I know you can do so much better than him.
Cause I see your bright light, he is trying to dim.

I know he's not a loving kind of man.
He's just a man I don't understand.

You see cause he does not care for you.
Cause he shows you that his love is untrue.

So why don't you get rid of that sorry excuse of a man?
And for yourself stand up and truly take a stand.

Test

You ran away so very fast.
You didn't wait to see if we could last.

You didn't try to pass this life's test.
I could have been to you the best.

You didn't even give us a try.
And I can't help but wonder why.

What about me scared you away?
Was it something that I did say?

I have so many questions in my heart.
That wasn't there at the beginning of our start.

I thought together we would be just fine.
I had no questions in my heart to not make you mine.

I guess this is just another life test.
So it's truly time to put this to rest.

Thinking of you

As I sit here thinking and my thoughts are of you.
And how I will love you with a love that is true.

My love for you will be pure genuine, and kind.
And you'll be the only man in my heart and on my mind.

I'm hoping that one day you will come to be mine.
And I'll show you that I will love you till the end of time.

Toy

You weren't very nice to me.
Now it's you I cannot see.

I have put you out of my mind.
Cause to me, you were not kind.

Now with you I am through.
Cause I want nothing else from you.

You were to me, not a man but a boy.
Cause with my heart, you did toy.

Now I've gotten away from you.
I'm so happy we are through.

Useless

Don't you know you deserve better than you have gotten?
Don't you know that man is useless and he is just rotten?

Don't you know you are a good woman, and you deserve better than that?
Don't you know he doesn't love you cause that's not where his hearts at?

Why are you turning a blinds eye and not looking at the warning sign?
Because he's been talking to you with words that are not kind.

He's showing you who he is, but you are looking the other way.
He's telling you who he is, with the unkind words he speaks each day.

Please pay attention to his word for his words are what they are.
Cause each unkind word will leave on your heart a significant scar.

He's shown you over and over again he's just not a good man.
Why do you choose to look the other way your heart doesn't understand.

You know this relationship will not end in the end in the right way.
But when it ends, you'll understand the words that I did say.

So I'm warning you to take heed to the words he does say.
Cause it's time for you to see him for who he is and walk away.

Victor

Hi, I didn't wake up next to you.
And there was nothing I could do.

I didn't ask for my life to change.
Now because of you my life feels strange.

Cause I wasn't trying to start something new.
And now I have too because of you.

You chose to make so quick an exit.
And you left me with my heart in a fit.

I'll learn from this lesson what I should know.
And I'll come out the victor and this I will show.

Warned

My neighbor warned me and warned me and warned me about you.
And if I would have listened all the pain I wouldn't have gone through.

I should have listened to the words she would say.
Maybe then you wouldn't have been in my heart's way.

She told me you weren't for me a good man.
But at the time, her words I didn't understand.

But what she said turned out to be true.
Because you really did put me through.

I wish I could go back to that moment in time.
And take heed to those words which are now mine.

Cause she was right about you with those words, she had said.
Cause now those words I can't get out of my head.

I wish I had listened to her words of concern.
Then this life's lesson I would not have had to learn.

What my heart couldn't see

What my heart couldn't see I don't understand.
Why you had to be such a really bad man.

I couldn't see that you weren't right for me.
Cause it was something plain to see.

You are a man who has so much pride.
But your lies you just couldn't hide.

There were so many lies you told.
But your lies managed to unfold.

I don't know why you were a bad man.
This I just can't begin to understand.

Now you can't accept why we are through.
All I can say is your going to have too.

What the heck

On you, I should have done a background check.
But when I thought about it, I said what the heck.

I thought to myself you I can trust.
Now when I look at you, all I see is disgust.

I never though I'd look at you this way.
But now the pain of you my heart does pay.

You've turned out to be such a horrible man.
A man now that I can barely stand.

That's why I must get away from you.
So I want you to know we are now through.

I have to get away before I lose all respect.
And before my life turns out to be a train wreck.

So far from you, I must go away.
So now that's It's over, you have a great day.

Without me

How can you be happy without me?
How good of a person I am you'll never see.

We could have been so good together.
Cause with me it doesn't get any better.

Cause I am a woman who is loving and kind.
And one who would have kept your heart in mind.

This woman you walked away from and made her cry.
Has a heart full of hurt because she doesn't know why.

You left me

You left me, and it hurt me so.
You left me, and my heart cried no.

You left me, and now my heart's in pain.
You left me, and now my heart has a stain.

You left me, and my world turned blue.
You left me, and I didn't know what to do.

You left me, and I felt so lost.
You left me, and my heart paid the cost.

You left me, and I do wonder why.
You left me, and my heart did cry.

You left me, so we are through.
You left me, now what shall I do.

Epilogue

Realism

Now that you have read my poetry and you've read some things about me.
I hope you understand how I am and who I am and how I've come to be.

I hope that in reading my poems, some of my words touched your heart.
And I hope and pray that they touched you, as your reading began to start.

So I hope that you may have found in it, somewhere words of encouragement.
And I hope you get my meaning of realism and love through the words I have sent.

So if you have found it engaging and an easy book to read.
Then to your mind and heart, I have planted a realism seed.

Thank you for reading

Thank you for taking out time to read my poetry.
I hope, in some way, you were inspired by me.

I hope you found most of my words, to be gentle and kind.
Cause these were words that laid heavy on my mind.

Some of my words, you might think, weren't very nice.
But some of my words were, somehow sweet as a spice.

But whatever you thought about my read.
I hope it somehow met you intellectual need.

Acknowledgement

With special thanks to Raeven, Ka'Shena, Sharon, for their assistance in editing the book and to my graphic designer, Destiny Brooke www. DBrookeDesigns.com.

About the Author

Patricia Lynn Turner is a native of Los Angeles, California. She is a mother, sister, grandmother, aunt and friend to many. She comes from a large family, who has always supported and admired her ability to use her gift of poetic writing. Patricia has often been called upon to express the emotions of family and friends through poetic prose for many various occasions. Throughout her lifetime, she has been commissioned to write to write for church programs and celebrations of life. Her poetry us unique, genuine and true to who she is, while inviting the reader to j experience life through her eyes.

Printed in the United States
By Bookmasters